Grade K

Scott Foresman

Reader's and Writer's Notebook

 PEARSON Glenview, Illinois • Boston, Massachusetts • Chandler, Arizona •
Upper Saddle River, New Jersey

ISBN 13: 978-0-328-47679-4
ISBN 10:   0-328-47679-X
18 19 20 V001 18 17 16 15

Listening and Speaking Rules ... 1–2

Unit 1: All Together Now

Week 1: The Little School Bus
Handwriting 3
Letter Recognition 4, 9
Decodable Story 5–6
High-Frequency Words 7
Conventions 8, 12
Comprehension 10
Writing 11

Week 2: We Are So Proud!
Handwriting 13
Letter Recognition 14, 19
Decodable Story 15–16
High-Frequency Words 17
Conventions 18, 21 24
Comprehension 20, 23
Writing 22

Week 3: Plaidypus Lost
Handwriting 25
Letter Recognition 26, 31
Decodable Story 27–28
High-Frequency Words 29
Conventions 30, 33, 36
Comprehension 32, 35
Writing 34

Week 4: Miss Bindergarten Takes a Field Trip
Handwriting 37
Letter Recognition 38, 43
Decodable Story 39–40
High-Frequency Words 41
Conventions 42, 45, 48
Comprehension 44, 47
Writing 46

Week 5: Smash! Crash!
Handwriting 49
Phonics 50, 55
Decodable Story 51–52
High-Frequency Words 53
Conventions 54, 57, 60
Comprehension 56, 59
Writing 58

Week 6: Dig Dig Digging
Handwriting 61
Phonics 62, 71
Decodable Story 63–64
Writing Process 65–66,
.... 69–70, 74, 77–80
High-Frequency Words 67
Conventions 68, 73, 76
Comprehension 72, 75

Unit 2: Look at Us!

Week 1: Flowers
Handwriting.............................. 81
Phonics 82, 87
Decodable Story 83–84
High-Frequency Words 85
Conventions.................86, 89, 92
Comprehension 88, 91
Writing 90

Week 2: Nature Spy ....
Handwriting.............................93
Phonics 94, 99
Decodable Story 95–96
High-Frequency Words 97
Conventions............. 98, 101, 104
Comprehension 100, 103
Writing 102

Week 3: Animal Babies in Grasslands
Handwriting......................... 105
Phonics 106, 111
Decodable Story 107–108
High-Frequency Words 109
Conventions............ 110, 113, 116
Comprehension 112, 115
Writing 114

Week 4: Bear Snores On
Handwriting.......................... 117
Phonics 118, 123
Decodable Story 119–120
High-Frequency Words 121
Conventions.......... 122, 125, 128
Comprehension 124, 127
Writing 126

Week 5: A Bed for the Winter
Handwriting.......................... 129
Phonics 130, 135
Decodable Story 131–132
High-Frequency Words 133
Conventions........... 134, 137, 140
Comprehension 136, 139
Writing 138

Week 6: Jack and the Beanstalk
Handwriting......................... 141
Phonics 142, 151
Decodable Story 143–144
Writing Process.............145–146,
.... 149–150, 154, 157–160
High-Frequency Words 147
Conventions........... 148, 153, 156
Comprehension 152, 155

Unit 3: Changes All Around Us

Week 1: Little Panda
Handwriting............................ 161
Phonics......................... 162, 167
Decodable Story 163–164
High-Frequency Words 165
Conventions.......... 166, 169, 172
Comprehension 168, 171
Writing 170

Week 2: Little Quack
Handwriting............................ 173
Phonics......................... 174, 179
Decodable Story 175–176
High-Frequency Words 177
Conventions........... 178, 181, 184
Comprehension 180, 183
Writing 182

Week 3: George Washington Visits
Handwriting............................ 185
Phonics......................... 186, 191
Decodable Story 187–188
High-Frequency Words 189
Conventions.......... 190, 193, 196
Comprehension 192, 195
Writing 194

Week 4: Farfallina and Marcel
Handwriting........................... 197
Phonics......................... 198, 203
Decodable Story 199–200
High-Frequency Words 201
Conventions........... 202, 205, 208
Comprehension 204, 207
Writing 206

Week 5: Then and Now
Handwriting...........................209
Phonics......................... 210, 215
Decodable Story 211–212
High-Frequency Words 213
Conventions............ 214, 217, 220
Comprehension 216, 219
Writing 218

Week 6: The Lion and the Mouse
Handwriting...........................221
Phonics.........................222, 231
Decodable Story 223–224
Writing Process............. 225–226,
............229–230, 234, 237–240
High-Frequency Words 227
Conventions........... 228, 233, 236
Comprehension 232, 235

Unit 4: Let's Go Exploring

Week 1: Rooster's Off to See the World
Handwriting...........................241
Phonics....................... 242, 247
Decodable Story........... 243–244
High-Frequency Words 245
Conventions...........246, 249, 252
Comprehension 248, 251
Writing 250

Week 2: My Lucky Day
Handwriting...........................253
Phonics....................... 254, 259
Decodable Story........... 255–256
High-Frequency Words 257
Conventions........... 258, 261 264
Comprehension 260, 263
Writing 262

Week 3: One Little Mouse
Handwriting...........................265
Phonics........................266, 271
Decodable Story........... 267–268
High-Frequency Words 269
Conventions........... 270, 273, 276
Comprehension 272, 275
Writing 274

Week 4: Goldilocks and the Three Bears
Handwriting...........................277
Phonics....................... 278, 283
Decodable Story........... 279–280
High-Frequency Words 281
Conventions...........282, 285, 288
Comprehension 284, 287
Writing 286

Week 5: If You Could Go to Antarctica
Handwriting...........................289
Phonics....................... 290, 295
Decodable Story........... 291–292
High-Frequency Words 293
Conventions........... 294, 297, 300
Comprehension 296, 299
Writing 298

Week 6: Abuela
Handwriting...........................301
Phonics........................302, 311
Decodable Story........... 303–304
Writing Process and Research........
305–306, 309–310, 314, 317–320
High-Frequency Words 307
Conventions............308, 313, 316
Comprehension 312, 315

Unit 5: Going Places

Week 1: Max Takes the Train

Handwriting...........................321
Phonics........................ 322, 327
Decodable Story 323–324
High-Frequency Words 325
Conventions...........326, 329, 332
Comprehension 328, 331
Writing 330

Week 2: Mayday! Mayday!

Handwriting...........................333
Phonics........................ 334, 339
Decodable Story 335–336
High-Frequency Words 337
Conventions........... 338, 341 344
Comprehension 340, 343
Writing 342

Week 3: Trucks Roll!

Handwriting...........................345
Phonics........................346, 351
Decodable Story 347–348
High-Frequency Words 349
Conventions...........350, 353, 356
Comprehension 352, 355
Writing 354

Week 4: The Little Engine That Could

Handwriting...........................357
Phonics........................ 358, 363
Decodable Story 359–360
High-Frequency Words 361
Conventions...........362, 365, 368
Comprehension 364, 367
Writing 366

Week 5: On the Move!

Handwriting...........................369
Phonics........................ 370, 375
Decodable Story 371–372
High-Frequency Words 373
Conventions...........374, 377, 380
Comprehension 376, 379
Writing 378

Week 6: This Is the Way We Go to School

Handwriting...........................381
Phonics........................382, 391
Decodable Story 383–384
Writing Process and Research........
385–386, 389–390, 394, 397–400
High-Frequency Words 387
Conventions...........388, 393, 396
Comprehension 392, 395

Unit 6: Putting It Together

Week 1: Building with Dad

Handwriting........................... 401
Phonics....................... 402, 407
Decodable Story 403–404
High-Frequency Words 405
Conventions........... 406, 409, 412
Comprehension 408, 411
Writing 410

Week 2: Old MacDonald had a Woodshop

Handwriting........................... 413
Phonics....................... 414, 419
Decodable Story 415–416
High-Frequency Words 417
Conventions............418, 421, 424
Comprehension 420, 423
Writing 422

Week 3: Building Beavers

Handwriting........................... 425
Phonics.......................426, 431
Decodable Story 427–428
High-Frequency Words 429
Conventions........... 430, 433, 436
Comprehension 432, 435
Writing 434

Week 4: Alistair and Kip's Great Adventure

Handwriting........................... 437
Phonics....................... 438, 443
Decodable Story 439–440
High-Frequency Words 441
Conventions........... 442, 445, 448
Comprehension 444, 447
Writing 446

Week 5: The House That Tony Lives In

Handwriting........................... 449
Phonics....................... 450, 455
Decodable Story 451–452
High-Frequency Words 453
Conventions........... 454, 457, 460
Comprehension 456, 459
Writing 458

Week 6: Ants and Their Nests

Handwriting........................... 461
Phonics.......................462, 471
Decodable Story 463–464
Writing Process and Research........
465–466, 469–470, 474, 477–480
High-Frequency Words 467
Conventions........... 468, 473, 476
Comprehension 472, 475

Name _____

Listening Rules

1. Face the person who is speaking.

2. Be quiet while someone is speaking.

3. Pay attention to the speaker.

4. Ask questions if you don't understand.

Name _____

1. Speak clearly.

2. Tell only important ideas.

3. Choose your words carefully.

4. Take turns speaking.

5. Speak one at a time.

Name _____

✏️ Color

🍎 **Directions:** Color the pictures that show settings for stories.

 School + Home

Home Activity: Ask your child to describe what he or she might do in the settings he or she colored.

Comprehension Setting **35**

Name _____

 **Draw**

At School	At the Pool

 Directions Draw pictures to show what you look like when you are at school and at the pool.

 Home Activity Ask your child to tell about each picture and to describe the way he or she looks at each place.

Name _____

 **Write**

T		

t		

| U | | |

| u | | |

| V | | |

| v | | |

 **Directions:** Have children write a row of each letter.

 Home Activity: Ask your child to show you how to write each letter.

Handwriting Letters *Tt, Uu,* and *Vv*   **37**

Name _____

 Circle

T 	G T F B	**t** 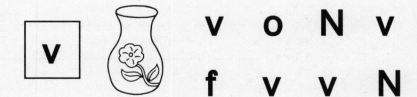 t f e t
	T F T D	a t b t
U	B D U E	**u** g u a b
	U G U U	u e c u
V	V N u V	**v** v o N v
	I n V V	f v v N

 Directions: Circle the letters that match the letter in the box.

 Home Activity: Have your child trace the letters and name the circled letters.

 Am I the little zebra?

Decodable Story *Am I Little?*
Letter Recognition *Tt, Uu, Vv, Ww, Xx, Yy, Zz*

Am I Little?

Am I the little turtle?

Am I the little van?

Am I the little

watermelon?

Name __OAKLYN o__

 **Write**  **Color**

12/1

the little

____the____ eee dog can sleep.

I have a ____little____ dog.

Did you feed ____the____ dog?

The ____little____ dog sleeps.

 Directions: Read each sentence. Write the missing word to finish the sentence. Color the picture.

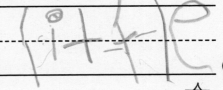 **Home Activity:** Have your child use *the* and *little* in other sentences.

© Pearson Education, Inc., K

Name _____

 Color 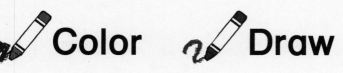 Draw

 Directions: Color the What We Can Do pictures in the top row. In the bottom row, draw pictures of other What We Can Do activities . Then tell about the things we can do.

 Home Activity: Ask your child to tell you about something he or she likes to do.

42 **Conventions** What We Can Do

Name _____

 Circle

 **Ww**   **W T F w f e w W**

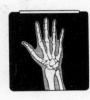 **Xx**   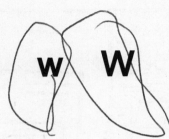 **B X D X x u d x**

 Yy    **Y X y v Y W y u**

 **Zz**    **x z Y Z X z V Z**

Directions: Circle the letters that match the letter in the box.

School + Home

Home Activity: Have your child trace and name the circled letters.

Name _____

 Circle  Color

 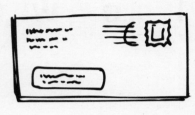  

 Directions: Circle items in each row that belong together. Color those pictures.

 Home Activity: Have your child draw three items that belong in a kitchen.

© Pearson Education, Inc., K

Name _____

Draw

Directions Draw pictures to show two characters on the field trip from the story.

School + Home
Home Activity Ask your child to name the characters and tell you about each one.

© Pearson Education, Inc., K

Name _____

 **Write**

cut	draw	paste

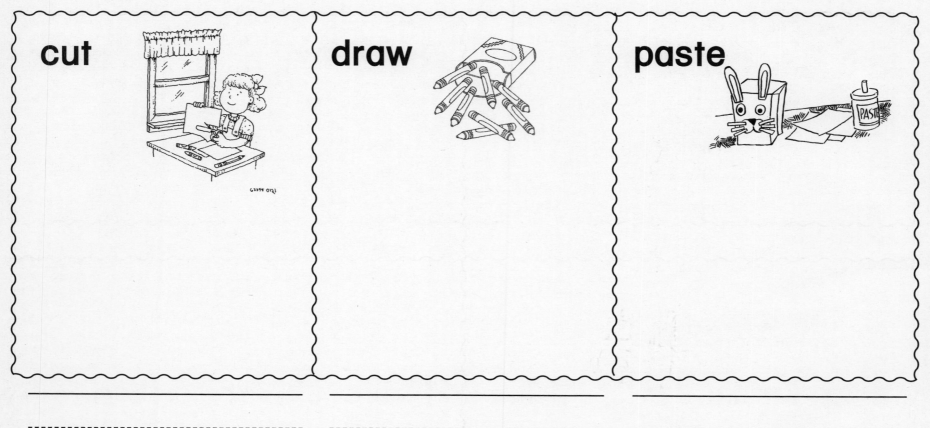

_____ _____ _____

- - - - - - - - - - - - - - - - - - - - - - - - - - - - - - - - - - - - - - - - - - - - -

_____ _____ _____

 Directions These are the words we use to give instructions. Write the word that goes with each picture to give instructions for making a rabbit.

 Home Activity Have your child tell how to make the rabbit.

Name _____

 Draw

 Directions Look at each story character. Draw a picture to show the story setting for that character.

 Home Activity Ask your child to name the characters and tell you about each one.

Comprehension Setting　**47**

Name _____

✏️ Draw

 Directions Draw pictures to show things you like to do. Then choose your favorite and tell about the favorite thing you like to do.

 Home Activity Ask your child to tell about other things he or she likes to do.

Name _____

✏️ **Write**

_____

_____

_____

_____

Mom ‾‾‾‾‾‾‾‾‾‾‾

_____

am ‾‾‾‾‾‾‾‾‾

_____

 Directions: Have children write a row of each letter and then write the words.

 Home Activity: Ask your child to show you how to write each letter.

Name _____

 Write Color

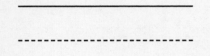

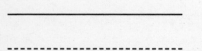

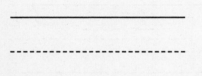   

Mm

   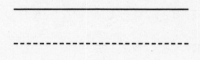

Directions: Name each picture. Write *m* on the line if the word begins with /m/. Color the /m/ pictures.

Home Activity: Have your child find pictures that begin with /m/ and paste the pictures on paper to make an /m/ book.

I walk to a little school.

Decodable Story *Little Mouse*
Target Skill /m/ Spelled *Mm*

Little Mouse

I am a little mouse.

I walk to a little school.

I am a little moose.

Name _____

 Write  Color

┌─────────────────────────┐
│   to   a   │
└─────────────────────────┘

_____

- - - - - - - - - - - - - - - - -

Tim has _____ map.

_____

- - - - - - - - - - - - - - - - -

Tim went _____ school.

_____

- - - - - - - - - - - - - - - - -

Pam went _____ school.

_____

- - - - - - - - - - - - - - - - -

Pam has _____ top.

 Directions: Read each sentence. Write the missing word to finish the sentence. Color the picture.

 Home Activity: Have your child use the high-frequency words in other sentences.

High-Frequency Words 53

Read It!

I see a boy.

Say It!

Say a sentence about something a dog does.

 # Write It!

_____

- -

I see a _____. (cat)

 Directions: Have children read the sentence about the boy with you. Ask them to give a sentence about a dog. Then have children write the word for an animal to complete the sentence.

 Home Activity: Ask your child to name other people and animals.

© Pearson Education, Inc., K

Name _____

 Write 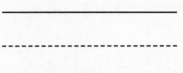 Color

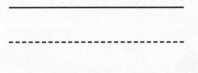 

Mm

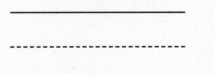

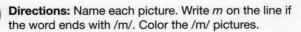

© Pearson Education, Inc., K

 Directions: Name each picture. Write *m* on the line if the word ends with /m/. Color the /m/ pictures.

 Home Activity: Have your child find an object at home that ends with /m/.

Phonics /m/ Spelled *Mm*   **55**

Name _____

 Color

Directions: Color the character in each box. Then tell about the character in each box.

 Home Activity: Ask your child to tell you about the characters in one of his or her favorite stories.

Name _____

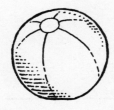 **Draw**

 Directions Draw pictures to show what you would do with the ball and the dog. Then tell what you are doing in each picture.

 Home Activity Have your child tell what he or she likes to do.

Conventions What We Can Do **57**

Name _____

 Write Color

_____
- -
_____

_____
- -
_____

Directions Write or dictate a caption for each picture. Color the pictures.

Home Activity Help your child create other captions for each picture.

School + Home

58 Writing Captions

Name _____

Number

 Directions: Number the pictures to show what happens first, next, and last.

 Home Activity: Ask your child to tell you how to do a task. Remind him or her to give the steps in the correct order.

Name _____

 **Read It!**

I see a cook.

Say It!

Say a sentence about

what a horse looks like.

 Write It!

_____

I see a _____. (bird)

Directions Have children read the sentence about the cook with you. Ask them to give a sentence about a horse. Then have children write the word for an animal to complete the sentence.

 Home Activity Point to each item. Have your child name the item and tell whether it is a person or an animal.

Name _____

✏️ Write

_____

- -

_____

- -

_____

Tom _____ **at** _____

Directions: Have children write a row of each letter and then write the words.

School + Home **Home Activity:** Ask your child to show you how to write each letter.

Handwriting Letters *T, t:* Words with *t* **61**

Name _____

  **Write** **Color**

 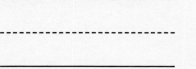 

  **Tt**

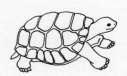

 Directions: Name each picture. Write *t* on the line if the word begins with /t/. Color the /t/ pictures.

 Home Activity: Have your child trace the target letter and name the pictures that begin with *Tt*.

I walk to a table.

4

Name _____

Tam!

I am Tam.

I am a turtle.

1

I walk to a tent.

2

I walk to a turkey.

3

Name _____

 **Draw**

Idea 1

Idea 2

Idea 3

 Directions Have children draw pictures of activities they do together as a class.

 Home Activity Ask your child to tell you about the activities in the pictures.

Name _____

 **Draw**

Our Story Idea

 Directions Have children draw a picture of the class's story idea.

 Home Activity Ask your child to tell you how the picture shows the class's story idea.

Name _____

 Write  Color

| to   a   little   am |

_____

- -

I am _____ cat.

_____

- -

I _____ a little cat.

_____

- -

I go _____ school.

_____

- -

The house is _____ .

Directions: Read each sentence. Write the missing word to finish the sentence. Color the picture.

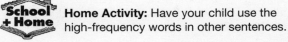 **Home Activity:** Have your child use the high-frequency words in other sentences.

Name _____

 ## Read It!

I see a book.

Say It!

Say a sentence that tells about your favorite book.

 ## Write It!

_____

- -

I see a _____. (park)

 Directions Have children read the sentence about the book with you. Ask them to give a sentence about the books in the picture. Then have children write the noun for a place to complete the sentence.

 Home Activity Ask your child to name other items that are places and things.

68 **Conventions** Nouns for Places and Things

Name _____

 **Draw**

Beginning   Middle   End

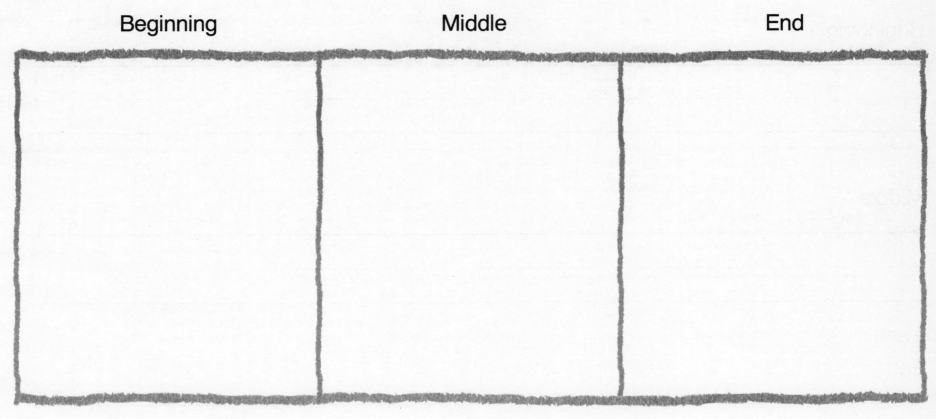

 Directions Have children draw pictures of the events for the beginning, middle, and end of the class story.

 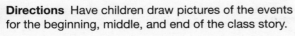 **Home Activity** Have your child tell you the sequence of events in the class story.

Name _____

✏️ **Write**

Beginning

_____

- -

_____

Middle

_____

- -

_____

End

_____

- -

_____

 Directions Have children write or dictate words or sentences that tell the beginning, middle, and end of the class story.

 Home Activity Ask your child to read the words or sentences to you.

Name _____

✏️ Write   🖍️ Color

_____

_____

_____

Tt

_____

_____

_____

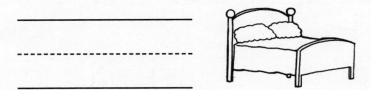

© Pearson Education, Inc., K

Directions: Name each picture. Write *t* on the line if the word ends with /t/. Color the /t/ pictures.

School + Home **Home Activity:** Have your child draw a picture of something that ends with /t/ and write the word.

Name _____

 Color

      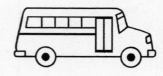   

 Directions: Color the pictures in each row that belong to the same group.

 Home Activity: Ask your child to sort toys into groups by color, size, or shape.

72 **Comprehension** Classify and Categorize

Name _____

 # Read It!

I see a girl.

Say It!

Say a sentence about the teacher.

 # Write It!

_____
- -

I see a _____. (hen)

Directions Have children read the sentence about the girl with you. Ask them to give a sentence about the teacher. Then have children write the word that names the animal to complete the sentence.

 Home Activity Ask your child to name other naming words (nouns) for people and animals.

Conventions Nouns for People and Animals **73**

Name _____

✎ **Draw**   ✎ **Write**

Details to Add

_____

- -

_____

- -

_____

- -

_____

 Directions Have children draw pictures or write words or sentences with details about the class story.

School + Home **Home Activity** Ask your child to explain how the details can be added to the class story.

Name _____

 Color

Directions: Look at the picture at the top of the page. Color the pictures in the boxes that are part of the setting.

 School + Home **Home Activity:** Have your child make up a story to go with the top picture.

Name _____

 **Read It!**

I see a house.

Say It!

Say a sentence that tells about a tree.

 **Write It!**

_____

- -

I see a _____. (bus)

 Directions Have children read the sentence about the house with you. Ask them to give a sentence about the tree in the picture. Then have children write the noun for a thing to complete the sentence.

 Home Activity Ask your child to name the items and then name other items that are places or things.

76 Conventions Nouns for Places and Things

Name _____

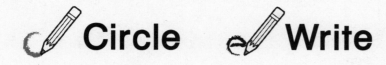 Circle ✏ Write

1. We like music.

_____

- -

_____

2. Thisis a new song.

_____

- -

_____

3. She plays forus.

_____

- -

_____

 Directions Have children circle the mistakes and rewrite the words or sentences correctly on the lines.

 Home Activity Ask your child to explain why correct spacing between letters and words is important.

Name _____

 Write

_____

- -

_____

- -

_____

- -

_____

- -

_____

- -

_____

Directions Have children copy sentences from the class story using correct spacing between letters and words.

 Home Activity Help your child edit the sentences by checking for correct letter and word spacing.

Name _____

 **Draw** **Write**

_____

- -

Title: _____

_____

- -

Author: _____

 Directions Have children draw a picture for a cover of their story. Help them write the story's title and their name.

 Home Activity Have your child explain how the picture and title go with the story.

Name _____

 **Circle**   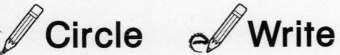 **Write**

_____

- -

I shared my story with _____.

Here's what he/she thought about my story.

_____

- -

_____

- -

_____

 Directions Have children circle the picture that shows with whom they shared their story. Then have children ask the peer or adult reviewer to fill in the blanks and to discuss the story with him or her.

 Home Activity Ask your child to read or tell the class story to you.

Name _____

✎ **Write**

_____
- -
_____

_____
- -
_____

_____
- - - - - - - - - - - - - - - - -
am _____

_____
- - - - - - - - - - - - - - - - -
at _____

 Directions: Have children write a row of each letter and then write the words.

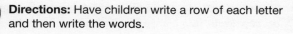 **Home Activity:** Ask your child to show you how to write each letter.

Name _____

 Write  Color

_____

- - - - - - - - - - - - - - - - - - - -

_____

_____

- - - - - - - - - - - - - - - - - - - -

_____

_____

- - - - - - - - - - - - - - - - - - - -

_____

Aa

_____

- - - - - - - - - - - - - - - - - - - -

_____

_____

- - - - - - - - - - - - - - - - - - - -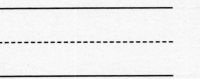

_____

_____

- - - - - - - - - - - - - - - - - - - -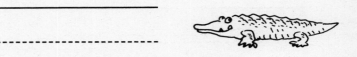

_____

© Pearson Education, Inc., K

 Directions: Name each picture. Write *a* on the line if the word begins with /a/. Color the /a/ pictures.

Home Activity: Have your child find other words that begin with /a/.

I have gum.

4

© Pearson Education, Inc., K

Decodable Story *I Have!*
Target Skill /a/ Spelled *Aa*

I Have!

I have a cat.

The cat is little.

1

I have a rat.

The rat is little.

2

I have a ham.

The ham is little.

3

Name _____

 Write  Color

have   is   little   am

_____
- -
Flowers _____ petals.

_____
- -
The flower is _____.

_____
- -
I _____ looking.

_____
- -
The girl _____ looking.

Directions: Read each sentence. Write the missing word to finish the sentence. Color the picture.

School + Home **Home Activity:** Have your child use the high-frequency words in other sentences.

© Pearson Education, Inc., K

Name _____

 **Read It!**

I see one hat.

Say It!

Say a sentence that tells how many hats you have.

 **Write It!**

_____

- -

I see two _____. (hats)

 Directions Have children read the sentence about the picture with you. Ask them to say a sentence that tells how many hats they have. Then have children write a word that means more than one to complete the sentence.

 Home Activity Ask your child to tell which word tells one and which tells more than one.

86 **Conventions** Nouns for More Than One

Name _____

 Write  Color

_____
- - - - - - - - - - - -
_____

_____
- - - - - - - - - - - -
_____

_____
- - - - - - - - - - - -
_____

Aa

_____
- - - - - - - - - - - -
_____

$1 + 1 = 2$

_____
- - - - - - - - - - - -
_____

_____
- - - - - - - - - - - -
_____

 Directions: Name each picture. Write *a* on the line if the word begins with /a/. Color the pictures with middle /a/.

 Home Activity: Have your child find an object at home that begins with *a*, draw a picture of it, and write the word.

Name _____

 Draw   Color

[top box — blank]

[bottom box — blank]

 Directions: Draw and color a daisy in the top box. Draw and color a tulip in the bottom box. Tell how your two flowers are alike and different.

 Home Activity: Have your child explain the similarities and differences between a daisy and a tulip.

Name _____

 **Read It!**

I see a school.

Say It!

Say a sentence that tells about a place you know.

 Write It!

_____

- -

I like to play _____. (ball)

Directions: Have children read the sentence with a noun that names a place. Ask them to say a sentence about a place they know. Then have children write a word to complete the sentence with a noun that names a thing.

 Home Activity: Have your child tell about places in your neighborhood. Then ask your child to name things found at home.

Name _____

 Write  Color

_____

- -

_____

- -

_____

- -

_____

 Directions: Write a label for each part of the picture. Color the picture.

90 Writing Labels

School + Home **Home Activity:** Help your child make labels for things around the house, such as *table, chair, door.*

Name _____

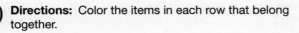 **Color**

 Directions: Color the items in each row that belong together.

© Pearson Education, Inc., K

 Home Activity: Name sets of three things and have your child tell you which two belong together and tell why: *knife, fork, book. Knife* and *fork* are silverware.

Comprehension Classify and Categorize   **91**

Name _____

 **Read It!**

I see three cats.

Say It!

Say a sentence that tells about things you have.

 **Write It!**

_____

- -

I have two _____. (bats)

 Directions: Have children read the sentence about the picture with you. Ask them to tell a sentence about things they have. Then have children write the noun for more than one to complete the sentence.

 School + Home **Home Activity:** Point to an item (or several items) and have your child name the item.

Name _____

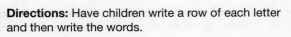 Write

_____

- -

_____

_____

- -

_____

_____   _____

-          -

Sam _____   sat _____

 Directions: Have children write a row of each letter and then write the words.

 Home Activity: Ask your child to show you how to write each letter.

Name _____

  Write  Color

_____

_____

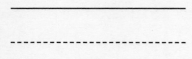

_____

_____

_____

_____

Ss

_____

_____

_____

_____

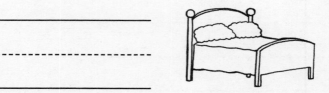

_____

_____

© Pearson Education, Inc., K

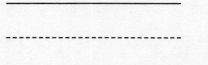 **Directions:** Name each picture. Write *s* on the line if the word begins with /s/. Color the /s/ pictures.

 **School + Home** **Home Activity:** Have your child find pictures that begin with /s/ and paste the pictures on paper to make a /s/ book.

94 Phonics /s/ Spelled *Ss*

I have the sock.

Decodable Story *Sock Sack*
Target Skills /s/ Spelled *Ss*

Name _____

Sock Sack

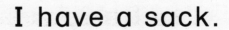

I have a sack.

The sock sack is little.

2

The sock is little.

3

Name _____

 Write  Color

have   is

_____
- -
I _____ to go to school.

_____
- -
This _____ the school.

_____
- -
I _____ to go home.

_____
- -
This _____ home.

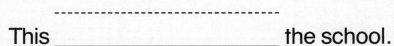

Directions: Read each sentence. Write the missing word to finish the sentence. Color the picture.

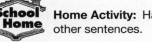 **Home Activity:** Have your child use *have* and *is* in other sentences.

Name _____

 Draw 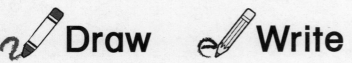 Write

 Directions: Draw pictures of a pet you know, a friend, and a family member. Use upper-case letters to write their names.

 Home Activity: Write the names of everyone in your family. Talk with your child about how people's first and last names use uppercase letters.

98 Conventions Proper Nouns

Name _____

 Write Color

_____

- -

_____

_____

- -

_____

_____

- -

_____

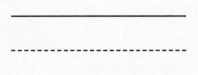

Ss

_____

- -

_____

_____

- -

_____

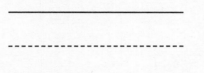

_____

- -

_____

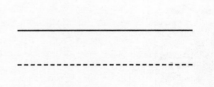

 Directions: Name each picture. Write *s* if the word ends with /s/. Color the picture if the word begins with /s/.

School + Home **Home Activity:** Have your child find an object that begins with the letter *s*, draw a picture of it, and write the word.

Phonics /s/ Spelled *Ss* **99**

Name _____

 Color  Draw

 Directions: Color the two pictures. Then in the last box draw a picture that tells where the story takes place.

 Home Activity: Have your child draw a picture of where the story takes place for one of his or her favorite stories.

100 **Comprehension** Setting

Name _____

 **Read It!**

I see two mats.

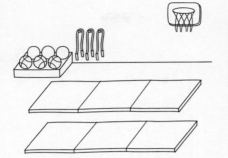

Say It!

Say a sentence that tells about things you have.

 **Write It!**

_____

- -

I see two _____. (cats)

Directions: Have children read the sentence about the picture with you. Ask them to tell about things they have in a sentence. Then have children write a word that means more than one to complete the sentence.

 Home Activity: Ask your child to draw other pictures that show more than one.

Name _____

 **Write**

 Directions: Make a list of three things from the book that you want to learn more about.

 Home Activity: Help your child write a list. It could be a grocery list or list of things to do.

© Pearson Education, Inc., K

Name _____

 Color

 Directions: Color the picture that shows what comes first in each story.

 Home Activity: Have your child draw three pictures to show how to feed a pet.

Circle  Write  Color

Mat
sat

_____

- - - - - - - - - - - - -

_____

mat
Tam

_____

- - - - - - - - - - - - -

_____

sat
Sam

_____

- - - - - - - - - - - - -

_____

 Directions Read the words and say the picture name. Circle the word that names the person in the picture. Then write the word and color the picture.

 Home Activity Help your child write the names for family members or friends and draw their pictures.

Name _____

 Write

_____

- -

_____

_____

- -

_____

_____

- - - - - - - - - - - - - - - - - -

Pam _____

_____

- - - - - - - - - - - - - - - - - - - -

pat _____

Directions: Have children write a row of each letter and then write the words.

School + Home

Home Activity: Ask your child to show you how to write each letter.

Handwriting Letters *P, p*: Words with *p*   **105**

Name _____

 Write   Color

_____

- - - - - - - - - - - - - - - - - - - -

_____

_____

_____

- - - - - - - - - - - - - - - - - - - -

_____

Pp

_____

- - - - - - - - - - - - - - - - - - - -

_____

_____

- - - - - - - - - - - - - - - - - - - -

_____

_____

- - - - - - - - - - - - - - - - - - - -

_____

Directions: Name each picture. Write *p* on the line if
the word begins with /p/. Color the /p/ pictures.

Home Activity: Have your child find pictures that
begin with /p/ and paste the pictures on paper to
make a /p/ book.

106   **Phonics** /p/ Spelled *Pp*

I like to pat Pam.

4

Decodable Story *Pat the Cat*
Target Skill /p/ Spelled *Pp*

Pat the Cat

I like to pat my cat.

1

 I pat my cat, Pam.

We pat Pam.

Name _____

 Write  Color

we   my   like

_____

We _____ the cat.

_____

We _____ my dog.

_____

_____ like to tap.

_____

_____ pig is little.

Directions: Read each sentence. Write the missing word to finish the sentence. Color the picture.

School + Home **Home Activity:** Have your child use *we*, *my*, and *like* in other sentences.

Name _____

 **Read It!**

I see a yellow sun.

Say It!

Say a sentence that tells about the sun.

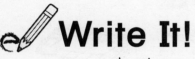 **Write It!**

_____

- -

I see a _____ sun. (round)

 Directions: Have children read the sentence about the sun. Ask them to say a sentence that tells about the sun. Then have children write the word that tells about the shape of the sun.

 Home Activity: Show pictures to your child and have him or her use color words and shape words to describe items in the pictures.

© Pearson Education, Inc., K

Name _____

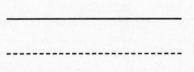 Write  Color

_____
- -
_____

_____
- -
_____

Pp

_____
- -
_____

_____
- -
_____

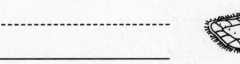

_____
- -
_____

_____
- -
_____

Directions: Name the pictures. Write *p* on the line if the word ends with /p/. Color the final /p/ words.

 School + Home **Home Activity:** Have your child use the final /p/ words in sentences.

Name _____

Color

 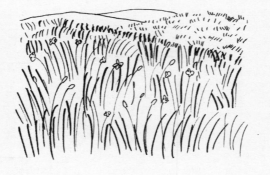 

Directions: Color the picture that tells what *Animal Babies in Grasslands* is all about.

School + Home **Home Activity:** Ask your child to tell you what the story is all about.

112 **Comprehension** Main Idea

Name _____

 Write Color

Pam

Sam

Pat

_____
- - - - - - - - - - - - - - - -
_____

_____
- - - - - - - - - - - - - - - -
_____

_____
- - - - - - - - - - - - - - - -
_____

Directions Write the name under each picture. Then color the pictures.

Home Activity Help your child make a list of names for pets and people.

Conventions Proper Nouns **113**

Name _____

 Write

trunk
big ears
tail

_____

- -

_____

- -

_____

Directions: Write a note about something you want to remember about the elephants.

School + Home **Home Activity:** Have your child make some notes about a favorite animal.

Name _____

 **Draw**

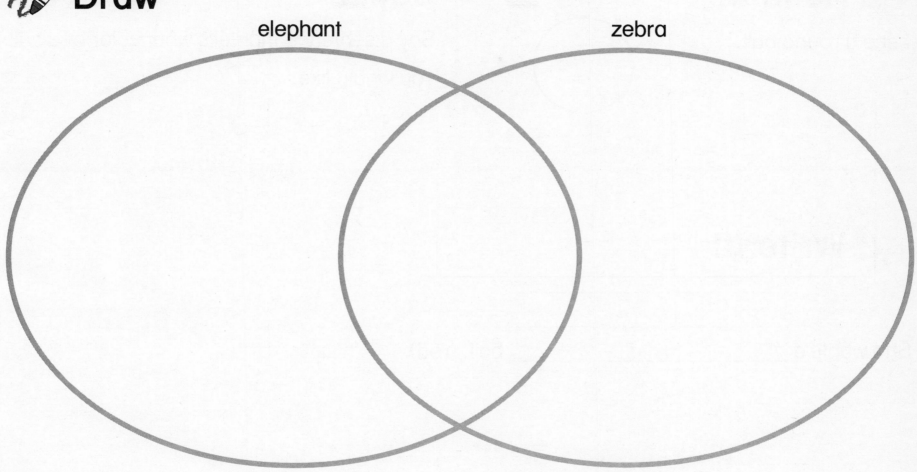

elephant   zebra

 Directions: In the left and right circles, draw pictures that show how the elephant and the zebra are different. In the space in the middle, draw a picture that shows how they are alike.

 Home Activity: While you eat a meal together, talk with your child about how the foods are alike and different.

Name _____

 **Read It!**

I see a round ball.

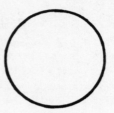

Say It!

Say a sentence that tells what color of a ball you would like.

 **Write It!**

_____

- -

She wants a _____ ball. (red)

 Directions: Have children read the sentence about the ball. Ask them to give a sentence that tells the color of the ball they would like. Then have children write the color word to complete the sentence.

 Home Activity: Help your child match items of the same shape or color and tell about the item—*I see a square table. I see a square book.*

Name _____

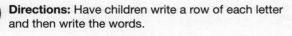 Write

_____

- -

_____

_____

- -

_____

_____

Cam _____

cap _____

 Directions: Have children write a row of each letter and then write the words.

School + Home **Home Activity:** Ask your child to show you how to write each letter.

Handwriting Letters C, c: Words with c   **117**

Name _____

 Write  Color

_____
- - - - - - - - - - - - - - - - - -
_____

_____
- - - - - - - - - - - - - - - - - -
_____

_____
- - - - - - - - - - - - - - - - - -
_____

 **Cc**

_____
- - - - - - - - - - - - - - - - - -
_____

_____
- - - - - - - - - - - - - - - - - -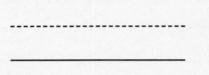
_____

_____
- - - - - - - - - - - - - - - - - -
_____

© Pearson Education, Inc., K

Directions: Name each picture. Write *c* on the line if the word begins with /k/. Color the /k/ pictures.

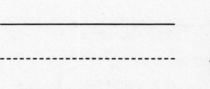 **Home Activity:** Have your child find an object at home that begins with /k/, draw a picture of it, and write the word.

118 **Phonics** /k/ Spelled *Cc*

The Cap

I have a cap.

We like the caps.

Decodable Story *The Cap*
Target Skill /k/ Spelled *Cc*

The cap is my cap.

2

I like my cap.

3

Name _____

 **Write**  **Color**

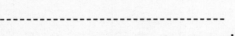
we   my   like

_____

It is _____ cat.

_____

_____ have a cat.

_____

We _____ the cat.

_____

We like _____ cat.

Directions: Read each sentence. Write the missing word to finish the sentence. Color the picture.

School + Home **Home Activity:** Have your child use *we, my,* and *like* in other sentences.

Name _____

 # Read It!

I see a big cap.

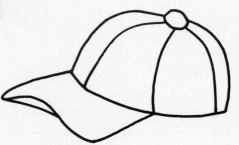

Say It!

Say a sentence that tells about the caps.

 # Write It!

_____

- -

I see two _____ caps. (little)

Directions: Have children read the sentence about the size of the cap. Ask them to give a sentence that tells about the caps. Then have children write the word that tells about the caps.

 Home Activity: Arrange pencils into groups by size. Have your child count and tell how many and what size.

122 **Conventions** Adjectives (Size and Number)

Name _____

 Write   Color

_____

- - - - - - - - - - - - - - - -

_____

_____

- - - - - - - - - - - - - - - -

_____

Cc

_____

- - - - - - - - - - - - - - - -

_____

_____

- - - - - - - - - - - - - - - -

_____

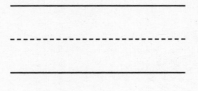

_____

- - - - - - - - - - - - - - - -

_____

Directions: Name each picture. Write *c* on the line if the word begins with /k/. Color the /k/ pictures.

School + Home

Home Activity: Have your child find other words that begin with /k/.

Phonics /k/ Spelled *Cc*   **123**

Name _____

 Circle 🖍 Color

 Directions: Circle the make-believe pictures. Color the real pictures.

 Home Activity: With your child, look at a book about how real animals live.

Name _____

 **Read It!**

I see a red book.

Say It!

Say a sentence that

tells about the hat.

 **Write It!**

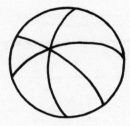

_____

- -

I see a _____ ball. (round)

 Directions: Have children read the sentence that tells about the book. Ask them to give a sentence that tells about the hat. Then have children write the word that tells about the shape of the ball.

 Home Activity: Have your child find things around the house that look like a circle, square, or triangle and tell about the shape and its color.

Conventions Adjectives (Color and Shape) **125**

Name _____

 **Write**  **Draw**

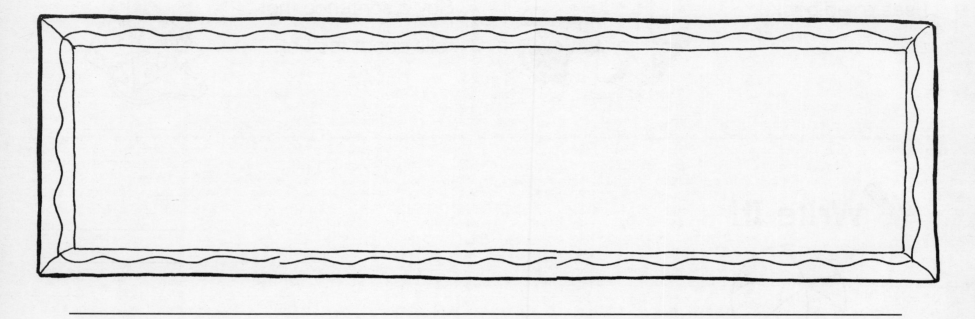

_____
- -
_____
_____
- -
_____

 Directions: Have children copy the class poem they wrote about the cat. Then have them draw a picture of a cat.

 Home Activity: Help your child make a poem with rhyming words such as *bat, cat. hat,* and *rat.*

Name _____

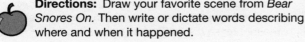 **Draw** **Write**

Directions: Draw your favorite scene from *Bear Snores On.* Then write or dictate words describing where and when it happened.

School + Home

Home Activity: Talk about or look at photographs of a favorite event with your child. Discuss where and when it happened.

Name _____

 # Read It!

I see two little cats.

Say It!

Say a sentence that tells about the cats.

✏️ Write It!

_____

- -

I see one _____ cat. (big)

 Directions: Have children read the sentence that tells about the size of the cats. Ask them to say a sentence that tells about the cats. Then have children write the word that tells about the cat.

 Home Activity: Gather a set of big and little books (or other items). Have your child choose the size and amount you say (1 little book).

128 **Conventions** Adjectives (Size and Number)

Name _____

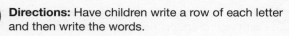 Write

_____

- -

_____

_____

- -

_____

- -

in _____

_____

- -

it _____

 Directions: Have children write a row of each letter and then write the words.

School + Home **Home Activity:** Ask your child to show you how to write each letter.

Handwriting Letters *I, i*: Words with *i* **129**

Name _____

 Write    Color

_____

- - - - - - - - - - - - - - - - - - - -

_____

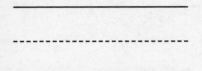

_____

- - - - - - - - - - - - - - - - - - - -

_____

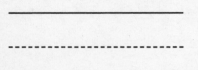

_____

- - - - - - - - - - - - - - - - - - - -

_____

 Ii

_____

- - - - - - - - - - - - - - - - - - - -

_____

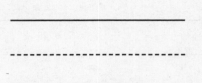

_____

- - - - - - - - - - - - - - - - - - - -

_____

_____

- - - - - - - - - - - - - - - - - - - -

_____

Directions: Name each picture. Write *i* on the line if the word begins with /i/. Color the /i/ words.

Home Activity: Look through a newspaper or book with your child and point out words that begin with *Ii*.

130 **Phonics** */i/ Spelled Ii*

He is a little pig.

4

Decodable Story *Tim the Pig*
Target Skill /i/ Spelled *Ii*

Name _____

Tim the Pig

Tim the pig is little.

1

Tim the pig can tap it.

Tim the pig can pat it.

Name _____

 Write Color

he   for

_____
- -
_____ has a pan.

The pan is _____ you.

_____
- -
_____ likes the pan.

It is _____ Pam.

Directions: Read each sentence. Write the missing word to finish the sentence. Color the picture.

Home Activity: Have your child write the words *he* and *for* using a fun material (yarn, sticks, glitter).

High-Frequency Words   133

© Pearson Education, Inc., K

Name _____

Read It!

I see a big house.

Say It!

Say a sentence that tells about the house.

 **Write It!**

_____ (soft   hard)

_____ (happy   sad)

 Directions: Have children read the sentence that tells about the house. Ask them to say a sentence that tells about the house. Then have children write the word that tells about each picture.

School + Home **Home Activity:** Ask your child to name the opposite of these words: *up, large, front, over.*

134 **Conventions** Adjectives (Opposites)

Name _____

 Write 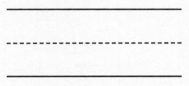 Color

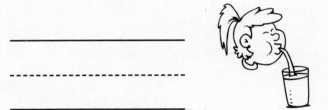

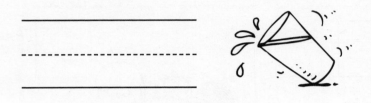

Ii

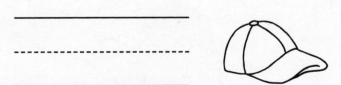

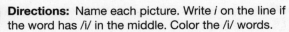

 Directions: Name each picture. Write *i* on the line if the word has /i/ in the middle. Color the /i/ words.

 Home Activity: Help your child make a list of words with /i/.

Name _____

 Number    **Color**

 Directions: Number the pictures to show what happened first, next, and last. Color the pictures.

 Home Activity: Have your child tell the steps to make something.

Name _____

 **Read It!**

I see a big pig.

Say It!

Say a sentence that tells about the pigs.

 **Write It!**

_____

- -

I see two _____ pigs. (big)

 Directions: Have children read the sentence that tells about the size of the pig. Ask them to say a sentence that tells about the pigs. Then have children write the word that tells about the pigs.

 School + Home **Home Activity:** Point to items in the house. Ask your child to name the size and number for the item.

Conventions Adjectives (Size and Number)   **137**

© Pearson Education, Inc., K

Name _____

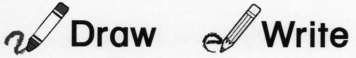 Draw Write

_____

- -

_____

 Directions: Draw a picture of an animal home. Then write a caption for your picture.

Home Activity: Point to pictures in a book or magazine and have your child think of a caption for each picture.

138 **Writing** Caption

Name _____

 Color

Directions: Color the items in each row that belong together.

 Home Activity: Name a category—animals, Ask your child to name things that fit the category.

Comprehension Classify and Categorize   **139**

Name _____

 **Read It!**

I see a little dog.

Say It!

Say a sentence that tells about the dog.

 Write It!

_____

- -

_____ (tall   short)

_____

- -

_____ (shut   open)

Directions: Have children read the sentence that tells about the dog. Ask them to say a sentence that tells about the dog. Ask children to write the word that tells about the picture on each line.

 School + Home

Home Activity: Have your child say the opposite of a word you name. Use words such as *up, back, over,* and *sad.*

Name _____

 Write

_____

- -

_____

- -

_____

_____   _____

- - - - - - - - - - - - - - -   - - - - - - - - - - - - - - -

in _____   it _____

_____   _____

- - - - - - - - - - - - - - -   - - - - - - - - - - - - - - -

pin _____   pit _____

 Directions Have children write a row of each letter and then write the words.

School + Home **Home Activity** Ask your child to show you how to write each letter.

Name _____

 Write   Color

p   n

m   p

s   p

c   t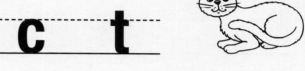

s   t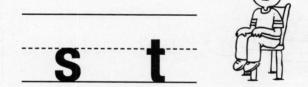

p   n

 Directions: Write *i* or *a* to finish each word. Color the /i/ pictures.

 Home Activity: Have your child write *tip* and *tap* and draw a picture for each word.

Sam, Sit!

Sit, pat, sip.

Sam, sit.

Decodable Story *Sam, Sit!*
Target Skill /i/ Spelled *Ii*

Sam, pat.

Sam, sip.

Name _____

 Draw

Idea 1	Idea 2	Idea 3

 Directions Have children draw pictures of children with plants that can do things real plants cannot.

 Home Activity Ask your child to tell you about what is happening in the pictures.

Name _____

Draw

Our Story Idea

 Directions Have children draw a picture of the class's story idea.

 Home Activity Ask your child to tell you how the picture shows the class's story idea.

146 **Writing Process** Planning

Name _____

 **Write**  **Color**

for   he

_____

- -

It is _____ Tim.

_____

- -

_____ has a bat.

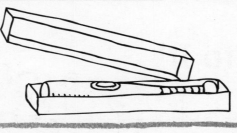

_____

- -

_____ can bat.

_____

- -

It is _____ Tim.

Directions: Read each sentence. Write the missing word to finish the sentence. Color the picture.

 Home Activity: Have your child use *for* and *he* in other sentences.

Name _____

 **Read It!**

I see a little kitten.

Say It!

Say a sentence that tells about kittens.

 **Write It!**

_____

I see _____ kittens. (two)

 Directions Have children read the sentence about the picture with you. Ask them to say a sentence that tells about kittens. Then have children write a word that tells how many to complete the sentence.

School + Home **Home Activity** Ask your child to name the color, shape, or size of things around the house.

Name _____

 **Draw**

Beginning	**Middle**	**End**

 Directions Have children draw pictures of the events for the beginning, middle, and end of the class story.

 Home Activity Have your child tell about the sequence of events in the story.

© Pearson Education, Inc., K

Name _____

 **Write**

Beginning

_____

- -

_____

Middle

_____

- -

_____

End

_____

- -

_____

 Directions Have children write or dictate words or sentences that tell the beginning, middle, and end of the class story.

 School + Home **Home Activity** Ask your child to read the words or sentences to you.

Name _____

 Write 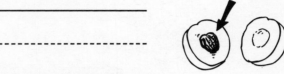 Color

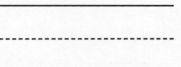

Ii

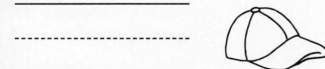

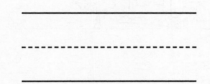

© Pearson Education, Inc., K

 Directions Name the pictures. Write *i* on the line if the word has /i/ in the middle. Color the /i/ pictures.

School + Home **Home Activity** Have your child draw a picture of something with /i/.

Phonics */i/* Spelled *Ii* **151**

Name _____

 Color  Draw

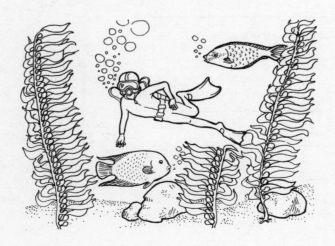

 Directions Color the picture that shows something make-believe. Draw something real in the box.

 Home Activity Read a favorite story with your child and talk about whether the story is make-believe or could really happen.

Name _____

 # Read It!

I see the hot sun.

Say It!

Say a sentence that tells about something cold.

Write It!

 _____

_____ (big   little)

_____

_____ (tall   short)

Directions Have children read the sentence that tells about the sun. Ask them to say a sentence that tells about something cold. Then ask children to say the picture name and read the words together. Have them write the word that tells about each picture.

 Home Activity Ask your child to name the opposite of these words: *light, day, small, down.*

Conventions Adjectives (Opposites) **153**

Name _____

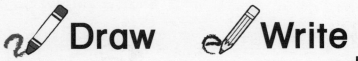 Draw  Write
Details to Add

 Directions Have children draw pictures or write words or sentences with details about the class story.

 Home Activity Ask your child to explain how the details can be added to the story.

Name _____

 Number

☐ ☐ ☐

☐ ☐ ☐

 Directions Number the pictures in each row to tell what happened first, next, and last.

 Home Activity Help your child tell about things he or she did, noting what happened in order.

Comprehension Sequence   **155**

Name _____

 **Read It!**

This is a little book.

Say It!

Say a sentence that tells about another book.

 **Write It!**

_____

- -

This is a _____ mouse. (little)

 Directions Have children read the sentence about the picture with you. Ask them to give a sentence that tells about a book. Then have children write the word that tells about the size of the mouse to complete the sentence.

 Home Activity Choose other words and have your child use the words to describe something.

156 Conventions Adjectives

Name _____

 Circle  Write

1. Look at that plant.

_____

- -

_____

2. That is a fastjig.

_____

- -

_____

3. Thegirl has fun.

_____

- -

_____

© Pearson Education, Inc., K

 Directions Have children circle the mistakes and rewrite the words or sentences correctly on the lines.

 Home Activity Ask your child to explain why correct spacing between letters and words is important.

Name _____

✏️ Write

_____

- -

_____

- -

_____

- -

_____

- -

_____

- -

_____

 Directions Have children copy the story sentences using correct spacing between letters and words.

 Home Activity Help your child edit the sentences by checking for correct letter and word spacing.

Name _____

 Draw 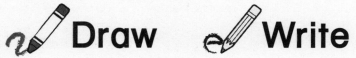 Write

Title: _____

Author: _____

 Directions Have children draw a picture for a cover
for their story. Help them write the story's title and
their name.

 Home Activity Have your child explain how the
picture and title go with the story.

Name _____

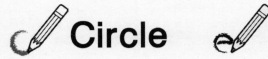 Circle  Write

I shared my story with _____.

Here's what he/she thought about my story.

_____

- -

_____

- -

 Directions Have children circle the picture that shows with whom they shared their story. Then have children ask the peer or adult reviewer to fill in the blanks and to discuss the story with him or her.

 Home Activity Ask your child to read or tell the class story to you.

Name _____

✏️ Write

_____
- -
_____

_____
- -
_____

_____
- - - - - - - - - - - - -
Nan _____

pan _____
- - - - - - - - - - - - -
_____

Directions: Have children write a row of each letter and then write the words.

School + Home **Home Activity:** Ask your child to write each letter and tell you how to make the letter.

Name _____

 Write    Color

_____

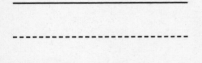

_____

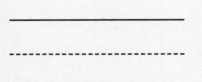

Nn

_____

_____

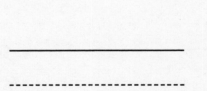

_____

 Directions: Name each picture. Write *n* on the line if the word begins with /n/. Color the /n/ pictures.

School + Home **Home Activity:** Have your child name other words that begin with /n/.

Nat sat.

Nan sat with Nat.

4

Decodable Story *Nan and Nat*
Target Skill /n/ Spelled *Nn*

Name _____

Nan and Nat

I am Nan.

I am Nat.

We have nets.

1

Nan is with Nat.

Nat can nab with a net.

Nat nabs with the net.

Nan nabs with the net.

Name _____

 Write  Color

she   with   me   we

_____

- -

Pam ran _____ me.

_____

- -

_____ like to run.

_____

- -

_____ ran to the mat.

_____

- -

Run with _____ .

Directions: Read each sentence. Write the missing word to finish the sentence. Color the picture.

School + Home **Home Activity:** Have your child use *me, with, she,* and *we* in other sentences.

Name _____

 Circle  Color

run

sit

net

dig

ball

hit

 Directions Name the pictures. Circle each verb and color the picture. Then use each verb in a sentence.

 Home Activity Have your child name other verbs.

166 Conventions Verbs

Name _____

 Write 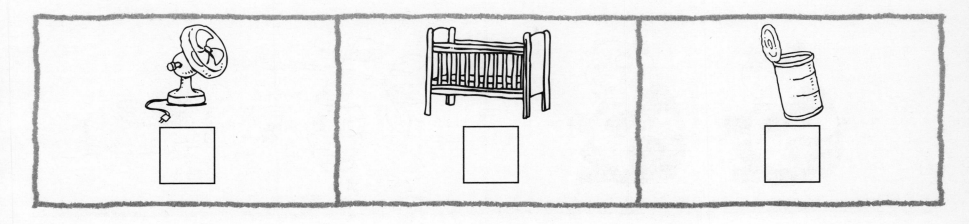 Color

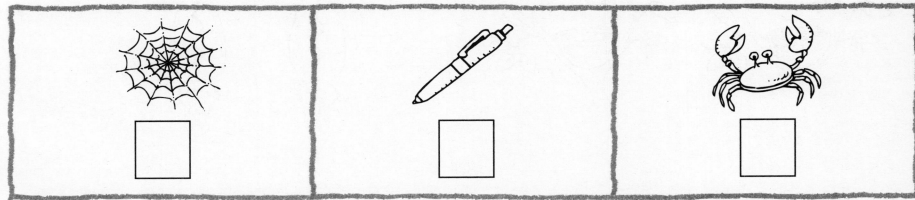

 Directions: Name each picture. Write the letter for the final sound in the box. Color final /n/ words green and final /b/ words blue.

School + Home **Home Activity:** Have your child trace *n* and *b* and name the pictures.

Phonics /n/ Spelled *Nn*, /b/ Spelled *Bb* **167**

Name _____

 Color

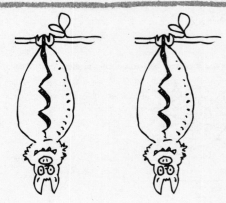

Directions Color pairs of pictures that are the same.

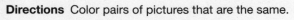 **Home Activity** Have your child tell how the pairs of pictures are alike or different.

Name _____

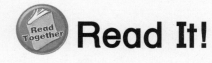 # Read It!

I see a little dog.

Say It!

Say a sentence that tells about dogs.

 # Write It!

_____

- -

I see a _____ cat. (white)

 Directions Have children track the print and read the sentence with you. Ask them to say a sentence that tells about dogs. Then have children write an adjective to complete the sentence.

 Home Activity Have your child describe things they see at home, telling about the size, color, and number.

Conventions Adjectives   **169**

© Pearson Education, Inc., K

Name _____

 Draw 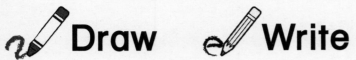 Write

Directions Draw a picture about Little Panda. Write or dictate words or sentences to tell about your picture and the selection.

 Home Activity Help your child summarize events that happened at school or at home.

Name _____

 Draw

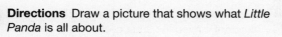 **Directions** Draw a picture that shows what *Little Panda* is all about.

 Home Activity: Talk about several familiar stories and have your child tell you what each story is all about.

Comprehension Main Idea **171**

Name _____

 Circle 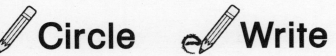 **Write**

pat

pit

_____

- - - - - - - - - - - - - - - - - -

_____

tap

tip

_____

- - - - - - - - - - - - - - - - - -

_____

nap

pin

_____

- - - - - - - - - - - - - - - - - -

_____

tan

sit

_____

- - - - - - - - - - - - - - - - - -

_____

 Directions Say the picture name. Circle the word that tells the action. Then write the word. Use each word you wrote in a sentence.

 Home Activity Ask your child to use the words that were not circled in sentences.

172 Conventions Verbs

Name _____

✏️ Write

_____

- -

_____

_____

- -

_____

_____

- - - - - - - - - - - - - - - -

Rin _____

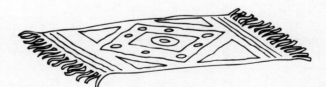

_____

- - - - - - - - - - - - - - - -

rat _____

 Directions: Have children write a row of each letter and then write the words.

 Home Activity: Ask your child to show you how to write each letter.

Name _____

 Write    **Color**

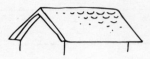

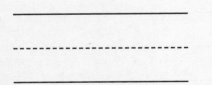 

Rr

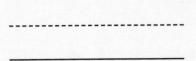

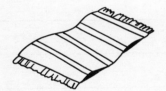

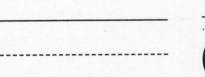

 Directions: Name each picture. Write *r* on the line if the word begins with /r/. Color the /r/ pictures.

© Pearson Education, Inc., K

 Home Activity: Have your child find pictures that begin with /r/ and paste the pictures on paper to make an /r/ book.

Rin ran to Rip.

Rip ran.

4

Decodable Story *Rin the Rat*
Target Skill /r/ Spelled *Rr*

Rin the Rat

Rin is a rat.

She is a little rat.

1

Rin likes to tap.

She can tap.

Rip ran to Rin.

He is with Rin.

Name _____

 **Write**  **Color**

| she   with   me   little |

_____

- - - - - - - - - - - - - - - - - - - -

_____ can jump rope.

_____

- - - - - - - - - - - - - - - - - - - -

She can run _____ me.

_____

- - - - - - - - - - - - - - - - - - - -

She can hop with _____ .

_____

- - - - - - - - - - - - - - - - - - - -

This is a _____ duck.

 Directions: Read each sentence. Write the missing word to finish the sentence. Color the picture.

 Home Activity: Have your child use *she, with, little,* and *me* in other sentences.

© Pearson Education, Inc., K

Name _____

 Read It!

Tim jumps.

Tim jumped.

Say It!

Say a sentence that tells something Tim is doing now. Then say a sentence that tells something Tim did yesterday.

 **Write It!**

_____

- -

Pam _____. (walks)

 Directions Have children read the sentences about Tim. Ask them to give sentences for things Tim does now and did yesterday. Then have children write the word that completes the sentence about Pam.

 Home Activity Ask your child to tell about something he or she did today and then about something he or she did yesterday.

178 **Conventions** Verbs for Now and the Past

Name _____

 Color  Write

🍎 **Directions:** Color each picture that begins with /r/. Write *r* in the box.

 School + Home **Home Activity:** Have your child name the pictures that begin with /r/.

Phonics /r/ Spelled *Rr* **179**

Name _____

 Draw

Directions: Draw a picture to show what would happen next in each story.

 School + Home

Home Activity: Ask your child to tell you the main events of the story *Little Quack*.

Name _____

✏️ **Draw**

run

sit

nap

rip

pin

tap

🍎 **Directions:** Draw a line from the word to the picture it tells about. Then use the verbs in sentences.

 Home Activity: Have your child use these verbs in sentences: *jump, hop skip, write.*

Name _____

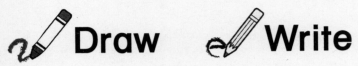 Draw  Write

Come to our class activity.

_____

- -

It is on _____.

_____

- - - - - - - - - - - - - - - - - - -

It is at _____ o'clock.

 Directions Draw a picture for your class activity. Then write or dictate the missing information for an invitation.

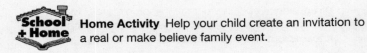 **Home Activity** Help your child create an invitation to a real or make believe family event.

182 **Writing** Invitation

Name _____

 Write  Color

 Directions: Label the animal in each picture *R* for real or *M* for make-believe. Color the pictures that show a make-believe situation.

 Home Activity: Have your child draw and color a picture of a real animal in a real place.

Comprehension Realism and Fantasy   **183**

Name _____

 **Read It!**

Nan talks.

Nan talked.

Say It!

Say a sentence that tells something Nan is doing now. Then say a sentence that tells something Nan did yesterday.

Write It!

_____

- -

Rob _____. (jumped)

 Directions Have children read the sentences about Nan. Ask them to give sentences for things Nan does now and did yesterday. Then have children write the word that completes the sentence about Rob.

 School + Home **Home Activity** Have your child create other sentences about the pictures.

Name _____

✎ Write

_____

- -

_____

- -

_____

Dad - - - - - - - - - - - -

did - - - - - - - - - - - -

Directions: Have children write a row of each letter and then write the words.

School + Home **Home Activity:** Ask your child to show you how to write each letter.

Name _____

 Write    **Color**

_____

- - - - - - - - - - - - - - -

_____

_____

- - - - - - - - - - - - - - -

_____

Dd

_____

- - - - - - - - - - - - - - -

_____

_____

- - - - - - - - - - - - - - -

_____

_____

- - - - - - - - - - - - - - -

_____

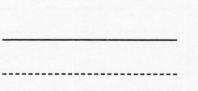

_____

- - - - - - - - - - - - - - -

_____

_____

- - - - - - - - - - - - - - -

_____

 Directions: Name each picture. Write *d* on the line if the word begins with /d/. Color the /d/ pictures.

 Home Activity: Have your child find pictures that begin with /d/ and paste the pictures on paper to make a /d/ book.

Pit ran to the dish.

Pit did.

4

Decodable Story *Pit Did!*
Target Skill /d/ Spelled *Dd*

Pit Did!

Pit can see the duck.

Pit ran with the duck.

Pit did.

1

Pit can see the doll.

Pit ran to the doll.

2

Pit can look at the door.

Pit ran to the door.

Pit did.

3

Name _____

 Write  Color

see   look

_____

I can _____ the cat.

_____

_____ at me!

_____

I _____ for my cat.

_____

Pat can _____ the dog.

Directions: Read each sentence. Write the missing word to finish the sentence. Color the picture..

School + Home **Home Activity:** Have your child use *see* and *look* in other sentences.

© Pearson Education, Inc., K

High-Frequency Words 189

Name _____

 **Write** 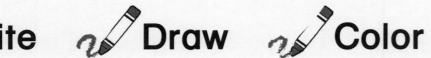 **Draw** **Color**

jump _____

_____

run _____

_____

walk _____

_____

 Directions: Add -s to each verb. Write the new word. Then draw a line to the picture that shows the action. Color each picture.

 Home Activity: Have your child use each verb in a sentence.

190 **Conventions** Verbs That Add -s

Name _____

 Write    Color

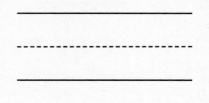

Kk
Dd

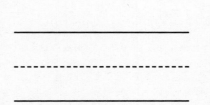

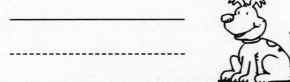

Directions: Name each picture. Write *k* on the line if the word begins with /k/ and *d* if it begins with /d/. Color the pictures.

 School + Home **Home Activity:** Have your child find other words that begin with /k/ or /d/.

Name _____

 Draw  Color

 Directions: Draw a line from what happened to why it happened. Color each picture.

 Home Activity: Have your child tell why each event happened.

192   Comprehension Cause and Effect

© Pearson Education, Inc., K

Name _____

 # Read It!

Tom packs.

Tom packed.

Say It!

Say a sentence that tells something Tom does now. Then say a sentence that tells something Tom did yesterday.

Write It!

walks
walked

_____

- -

_____

looks
looked

_____

- -

_____

 Directions Have children read the sentences about Tom. Ask them to give sentences for things Tom does now and did yesterday. Then have children write the word that tells about each picture.

 Home Activity Have your child use the words in sentences.

Conventions Verbs for Now and the Past   **193**

Name _____

 Draw ✏️ Write

Directions Draw a picture of something you like. Write or dictate words or sentences that would help someone else like it.

Home Activity Help your child tell about something he or she likes and how he or she would try to convince someone to like the same thing .

194 **Writing** Persuasive Statements

Name _____

 **Draw**

dog   cat

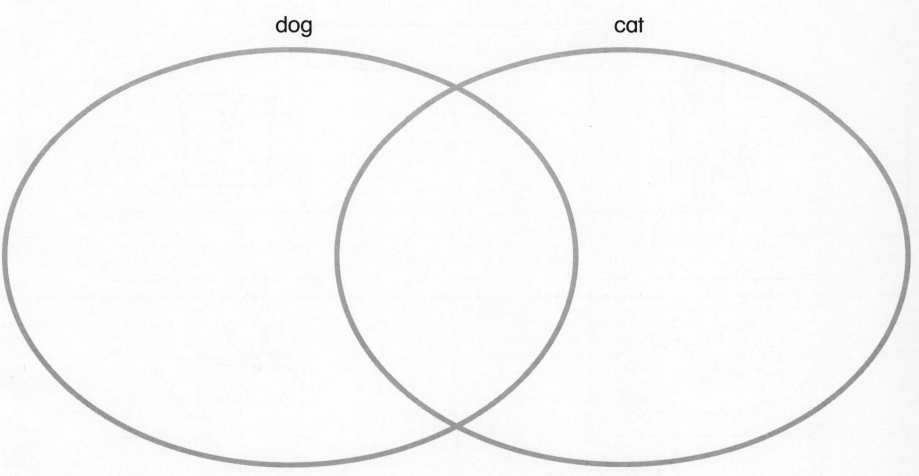

 © Pearson Education, Inc., K

Directions: In the left and right circles, draw pictures that show how a dog and a cat are different. In the space in the middle, draw a picture that shows how they are alike.

School + Home **Home Activity:** Have children explain the similarities and differences between two books.

Name _____

 **Write**

nap   rip   sit   tip

_____

- - - - - - - - - - - - - - - - - - -

_____

_____

- - - - - - - - - - - - - - - - - - -

_____

_____

- - - - - - - - - - - - - - - - - - -

_____

_____

- - - - - - - - - - - - - - - - - - -

_____

 Directions Add an -s to the verb at the top of the page and write the word that names each picture.

 Home Activity Help your child use the words in sentences.

196 **Conventions** Verbs That Add -s

Name _____

 **Write**

_____

- -

_____

_____

- -

_____

Fin - - - - - - - - - - - - - - - - - -   **fit** - - - - - - - - - - - - - - - -

 Directions: Have children write a row of each letter and then write the words.

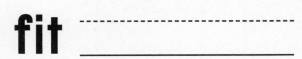 **Home Activity:** Ask your child to show you how to write each letter.

Handwriting Letters *F, f:* Words with *f*   **197**

Name _____

 Write  Color

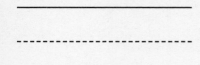

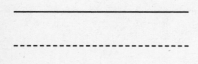

Ff

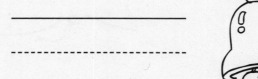

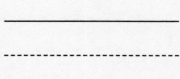

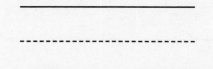

 Directions: Name each picture. Write *f* on the line if the word begins with /f/. Color the /f/ pictures.

School + Home **Home Activity:** Have your child find pictures that begin with /f/ and paste the pictures on paper to make a /f/ book.

I see a fin for me.

Look at the fin.

Decodable Story *For Me!*
Target Skill /f/ Spelled *Ff*

For Me!

I see a fan for me.

Look at the fan.

I see a fox for me.

Look at the little fox.

I see a fish for me.

Look at the little fish.

2

3

Name _____

 **Write**    **Color**

| see | look | with | for |

_____
- -
I can _____ the bird.

_____
- -
I can _____ for it.

_____
- -
It is _____ the cat.

_____
- -
Mom can run _____ me.

 **Directions:** Read each sentence. Write the missing word to finish the sentence. Color the picture.

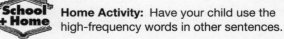 **Home Activity:** Have your child use the high-frequency words in other sentences.

© Pearson Education, Inc., K

High-Frequency Words   201

Name _____

 **Read It!**

Ann sits.

Ann will sit.

Say It!

Say a sentence that tells something Ann does now. Then say a sentence that tells something Ann will do tomorrow.

 **Write It!**

_____

- -

Ed _____. (will look)

 Directions Have children read the sentences about Ann. Ask them to give sentences for things Ann does now and will do in the future. Then have children write the words that complete the sentence about Ed.

 Home Activity Have your child tell about things that are happening now and things that will happen in the future.

Name _____

 **Color**   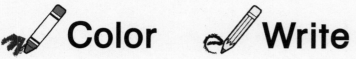 **Write**

Directions: Name the pictures. Color each picture that begins with /f/. Write *f* in the box.

Home Activity: Have your child name the pictures that begin with /f/.

Phonics /f/ Spelled *Ff*   **203**

Name _____

 Number

 Directions: Number the pictures 1, 2, and 3 to tell the beginning, middle, and end of *Farfallina & Marcel*.

 Home Activity: Have your child tell what happens at the beginning, middle, and end of the story.

Name _____

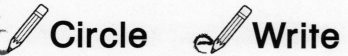 Circle  Write

hop   hops

_____

Pam _____ to me.

sit   sits

_____

Tim _____ in it.

pat   pats

_____

Nan _____ the cat.

 Directions Circle the word that completes the sentence. Write the word.

School + Home **Home Activity** Have your child create new sentences for the word choices.

© Pearson Education, Inc., K

Conventions Verbs That Add -s   **205**

Name _____

Draw   Write

_____
- -
_____
- -
_____
- -
_____

Directions Draw a picture of an animal in the box. Write or dictate a caption for your picture .

 Home Activity Look at pictures in a magazine and have your child provide a caption for each picture.

Name _____

 **Color**

 Directions Color the pictures of the two characters in the story.

 Home Activity Have your child tell you about the two story characters, Farfallina and Marcel.

© Pearson Education, Inc., K

Name _____

Read It!

Kim hops.

Kim will hop.

Say It!

Say a sentence that tells something you are doing now. Then say a sentence that tells something you will do tomorrow.

Write It!

_____

The man _____. (will run)

 Directions Have children read the sentences about Kim. Ask them to give sentences for things they do now and things they will do tomorrow. Then have children write the words that complete the sentence about the man.

 Home Activity Have your child create sentences using the words on the page.

Name _____

 Write

_____

- -

_____

- -

_____

Otto - - - - - - - - - - - - - -   **odd** - - - - - - - - - - - - - - -

🍎 **Directions:** Have children write a row of each letter and then write the words.

 Home Activity: Ask your child to show you how to write each letter.

Name _____

 Write  Color

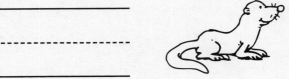

 Oo

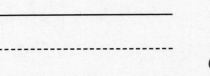

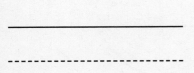

Directions: Name each picture. Write *o* on the line if the word begins with /o/. Color the /o/ pictures.

© Pearson Education, Inc., K

School + Home **Home Activity:** Look through a newspaper or book with your child and point out words that begin with /o/.

Little Rob is not sad.

Little Rob can have the top.

4

Decodable Story *Little Rob*
Target Skill /o/ Spelled *Oo*

Little Rob

Little Rob is sad.

He is little.

1

Little Rob is on a mat.

He is sad.

Little Rob can see a top.

Can he have the top?

Name _____

 **Write**   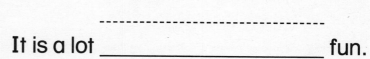 **Color**

| they | of | you | she |

_____

Can _____ see you?

_____

It is a lot _____ fun.

_____

Can _____ see the top?

_____

_____ can see the fox.

 Directions: Read each sentence. Write the missing word to finish the sentence. Color the picture.

School + Home **Home Activity:** Have your child use the high-frequency words in other sentences.

High-Frequency Words   213

Name _____

Read  Draw

We have a bat.

Rob can mop.

It is a fan.

 Directions: Read each sentence. Draw a picture that shows the meaning of word group.

 Home Activity: Have your child read the meaningful word groups and tell about his or her pictures.

214 **Conventions** Meaningful Word Groups

Name _____

 Write   Color

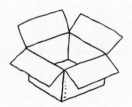

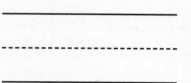

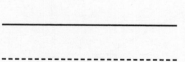

 Directions: Name each picture. Write *o* on the line if the word has /o/ in the middle. Color the /o/ pictures.

 Home Activity: Help your child make a list of words with /o/.

Name _____

 Circle  Color

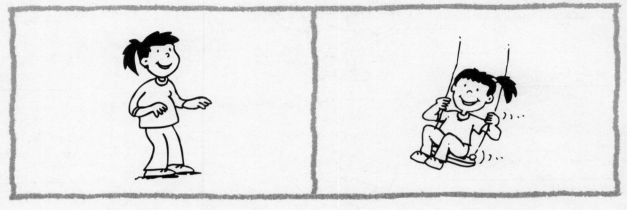

 Directions: Circle the picture that shows what you think the child would do next. Color the picture

 Home Activity: Have your child explain how he or she arrived at his or her conclusion.

Name _____

 # Read It!

Dan will see the bird.

Dan sees the bird.

Say It!

Say a sentence that tells something you can see now. Then say a sentence that tells something you might see tomorrow.

Write It!

The girl _____ the apple. (will eat)

Directions Have children read the sentences about Dan. Ask them to give sentences for things they see now and things they will see tomorrow. Then have children write the words that complete the sentence about the girl.

 School + Home **Home Activity** Have your child use the action words in sentences.

Conventions Verbs for Now and the Future **217**

Name _____

✏️ Write

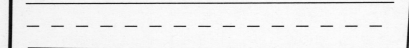

1. _____

2. _____

3. _____

🍎 **Directions** After listening to class discussions about now and the past, take notes by writing or dictating a list of things from the past that you want to learn more about.

 Home Activity Help your child write a list of things to do on a rainy day.

Name _____

Draw   Color

 Directions: Compare and contrast a bicycle and a car. Draw the slower thing in the top box and color it. Draw the faster thing in the bottom box and color it. Tell how the two things are alike and different.

 Home Activity: Ask children how a bicycle and a car are alike and different.

Comprehension Compare and Contrast   **219**

Name _____

 **Draw**

We have a top.

I see a cat.

Look at the map.

Directions Draw a line from the word group to the picture it tells about. Then point to a picture and tell something about it.

School + Home **Home Activity** Point to things around the house and have your child create a meaningful word group about each item.

Name _____

**Write**

_____

- -

_____

_____

- -

_____

top _____
- - - - - - - - - - - - -
_____

cot - - - - - - - - - - - - -
_____

mop _____
- - - - - - - - - - - - -
_____

dot - - - - - - - - - - - - -
_____

© Pearson Education, Inc., K

Directions: Have children write a row of each letter and then write the words.

Home Activity: Ask your child to show you how to write each letter.

Name _____

 Write  Color

f **x**

t **p**

c **p**

O o

m **p**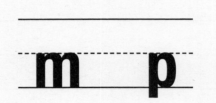

b **b**

b **x**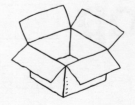

 Directions: Write *o, a,* or *i* to finish each word. Color the /o/ pictures.

 **Home Activity:** Have your child write *mop* and *map* and draw a picture for each word.

222 **Phonics** /o/ Spelled *Oo*

It is not on the rat.

It is in the pot.

4

Decodable Story *A Cap for Tom*
Target Skill /o/ Spelled *Oo*

A Cap for Tom

Tom can have a cap.

Is the cap on Tom?

1

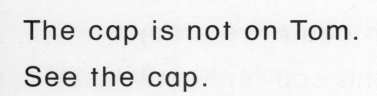

The cap is not on Tom.

See the cap.

2

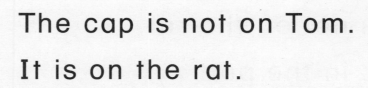

The cap is not on Tom.

It is on the rat.

3

Name _____

 Write

Lion

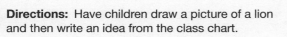 **Directions:** Have children draw a picture of a lion and then write an idea from the class chart.

 Home Activity: Ask your child to tell you about the picture.

© Pearson Education, Inc., K

Name _____

 **Draw** 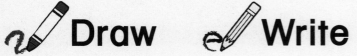 **Write**

Mouse

 Directions: Have children draw a picture of a mouse and then write an idea from the class chart.

School + Home **Home Activity:** Ask your child to explain the class's ideas for a poem.

226 **Writing Process** Planning

Name _____

 Write  Color

| they | of | you | we |

_____

_____ can see the dog.

_____

I see a lot _____ dogs.

_____

They can run to _____ .

_____

_____ ran to me.

Directions: Read each sentence . Write the missing word to finish the sentence. Color the picture.

School + Home **Home Activity:** Have your child use the high-frequency words in other sentences.

Name _____

 **Draw**

Ron can see the rod.

Mop pin is my.

Mom is at the top.

 Directions: Read each group of words. If the words make a sentence, draw a picture that shows the meaning of the sentence.

 Home Activity: Have your child read each group of words and tell which words do not make a sentence.

228 **Conventions** Sentences

Name _____

✏️ Draw

Beginning	Middle	End

Directions: Have children draw pictures of the events for the beginning, middle, and end of the class poem.

School + Home

Home Activity: Have your child tell you the sequence of events in the class poem.

Name _____

 **Write**

Beginning

_____

_____

Middle

_____

_____

End

_____

_____

© Pearson Education, Inc., K

 Directions Have children write or dictate words and sentences about the events for the beginning, middle, and end of the class poem.

  School + Home **Home Activity** Ask your child to read the words or sentences to you..

Name _____

 Circle  Color

fix fox		map mop	
cab cob		tap top	

Directions: Circle the word that names the picture.
Color the /o/ pictures.

School + Home **Home Activity:** Have your child draw a picture of an /o/ word.

Phonics /o/ Spelled *Oo* **231**

Name _____

 Color

Directions: Color the picture that shows the main idea of the story *The Lion and the Mouse*.

 Home Activity: Have your child tell what lesson the lion learned from the mouse.

© Pearson Education, Inc., K

Name _____

✏️ **Circle**

Pam got a cap.

Pam got a top.

Tom had a map.

Tom had a mat.

Nan sat.

Nan ran.

Tim ran to Tom.

Tim ran to Pam.

 Directions Circle the words that tell about the picture .

 Home Activity Have your child read the word groups to you and tell about the pictures.

Conventions Meaningful Word Groups **233**

Name _____

 Draw  Write

Details to Add

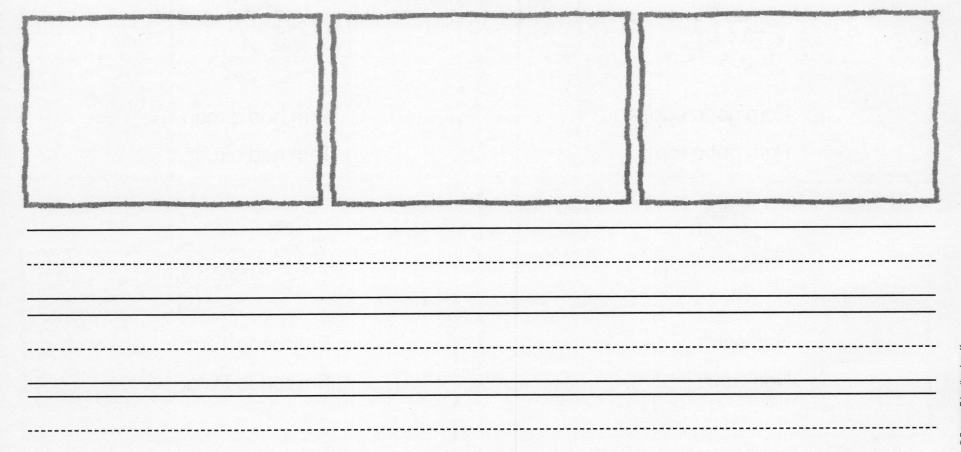

_____

- -

_____

- -

_____

- -

 Directions Have children draw pictures or write words or sentences with details about the class poem.

 Home Activity Ask your child to explain how the details can be added to the class poem.

234 **Writing Process** Revising

Name _____

 Number  **Color**

 Directions: Number the pictures in each row to tell what happened first, next, and last. Color the pictures.

 Home Activity: Help your child tell about things he or she did, noting what happened in order.

© Pearson Education, Inc., K

Name _____

✏️ **Circle**

Pam can pat the cat.

Pam the cat can.

mat Sam on sat.

Sam sat on the mat.

A little got Nan.

Nan got a little cap.

The man sat.

Sat man the.

🍎 **Directions** Circle the words that make a sentence that tells about the picture.

 Home Activity Ask your child to create another sentence for each picture.

Name _____

 Circle 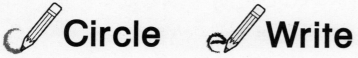 Write

1. the mouse is s c a r e d .

_____

- -

_____

2. he isnow a big   lion.

_____

- -

_____

3. they   willbe friends.

_____

- -

_____

 Directions Have children circle the mistakes and rewrite the words or sentences correctly on the lines.

 Home Activity Ask your child to explain how he or she fixed the mistakes in the sentences.

Writing Process Editing **237**

Name _____

 Write

_____

- -

_____

- -

_____

- -

_____

- -

_____

Directions Have children copy sentences from the class poem using correct spacing between letters and words and correct capitalization.

 Home Activity Help your child edit the sentences by checking for correct letter and word spacing and capitalization.

Name _____

✏️ Draw ✏️ Write

Title: _____

Author: _____

 Directions Have children draw a picture for a cover for their poem. Help them write the poem's title and their name.

 Home Activity Have your child explain how the picture and title go with the poem.

Name _____

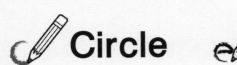 Circle  Write

_____

- -

I shared my poem with _____.

Here's what he/she thought about my poem.

_____

- -

_____

- -

_____

 Directions Have children circle the picture that shows with whom they shared their poem. Then have children ask the peer or adult reviewer to fill in the blanks and to discuss the poem with him or her.

 School + Home **Home Activity** Ask your child to read or tell the class poem to you.

Name _____

 Write

_____
- -
_____

_____
- -
_____

_____
- - - - - - - - - - - - - -
Hob _____

_____
- - - - - - - - - - - - - -
Hat _____

Directions: Have children write a row of each letter and then write the words.

 School + Home

Home Activity: Ask your child to write each letter and tell you how to make the letter.

Handwriting Letters *H, h*: Words with *h*   **241**

Name _____

 Write    Color

_____
- - - - - - - - - - - - - -
_____
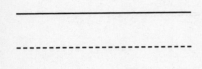

_____
- - - - - - - - - - - - - -
_____
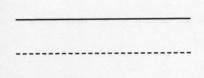

_____
- - - - - - - - - - - - - -
_____

Hh

_____
- - - - - - - - - - - - - -
_____

_____
- - - - - - - - - - - - - -
_____
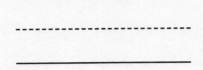

_____
- - - - - - - - - - - - - -
_____

Directions: Name the pictures. Write *h* on the line if the word begins with /h/. Color the /h/ pictures.

School + Home **Home Activity:** Have your child find other words with /h/ such as *hat*.

I like my hat.

Do you like my hat?

4

Decodable Story *I Have!*
Target Skill /h/ Spelled *Hh*

I Have!

I have a hat.

The hat is little.

That is my hat.

1

The hat is on me.

It is my little hat.

Do you have a little hat?

I can hop with the hat.

I can hit with the hat.

Name _____

 Write    Color

| are | that | do |

_____

- - - - - - - - - - - - - - - - - - - -

_____ they little?

_____

- - - - - - - - - - - - - - - - - - - -

We _____ little.

_____ you like cats?

_____ is a little hat.

 Directions: Write the missing word to finish each sentence. Color the pictures.

School + Home **Home Activity:** Have your child use the high-frequency words in other sentences.

Name _____

 Circle  Color

The cat can hit.

The bat hid on the top.

Hob can see the top.

A man sat on the mat.

 Directions: Circle the naming part of each sentence. Color the naming part in the picture. Use the naming part in a sentence of your own.

 Home Activity: Help your child create a sentence using these namng parts: *the dog, a rooster, my friend, some people.*

246 **Conventions** Naming Parts

Name _____

 Write  Color

Hh

 Directions: Name each picture. Write the letter for the beginning sound. Color the /h/ pictures.

Home Activity: Have your child write rhyming /h/ words for the words *cat*, *top*, and *sit* and then draw a picture for each word.

Phonics /h/ Spelled *Hh* **247**

Name _____

 Number  Color

 Directions: Number the pictures 1, 2, and 3 to tell what happened first, next, and last. Have children retell the sequence using the words *first, next,* and *last.* Then have them color the pictures.

 Home Activity: Have your child tell the steps to draw a picture.

248 **Comprehension** Sequence

Name _____

 **Circle**

Hat have little.

I have a hat.

Hob can hit it.

It can Hob.

The on the hat.

The cat sat on the hat.

That hat is little.

Little is hat.

 Directions: Circle the words that make a sentence that tell about the picture. Help children tell why the words they chose make a complete sentence.

 Home Activity: Ask your child to create another sentence for each picture.

Name _____

✏️ Write

Walk	Turn	Stop
		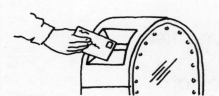

_____   _____   _____

- -

_____   _____   _____

🍎 **Directions** Give directions to go to the mailbox.
Write the word for each picture.

🏠 School + Home **Home Activity** Help your child read the words to give
directions for mailing a letter.

250 **Writing** Directions

Name _____

 Color

Directions: Color the pictures that are alike in each row. Tell how the pictures are alike.

 School + Home **Home Activity:** Have your child tell how the pictures are alike and how they are different.

Comprehension Compare and Contrast **251**

Name _____

 **Circle**    **Color**

A fan is by the mat.

The pet is mad.

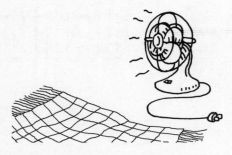

The cat ran to the man.

The rat is on the top .

 Directions: Read the sentence. Circle the naming part of the sentence. Then color the naming part in the picture. Use the naming part in a sentence of your own.

 Home Activity: Ask your child to read the sentence and tell the naming part .

Name _____

 Write

_____
- -
_____

_____
- -
_____

_____
- - - - - - - - - - - - - - - - -

Lad _____

lid _____

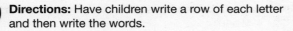 **Directions:** Have children write a row of each letter and then write the words.

 Home Activity: Ask your child to show you how to write each letter.

Handwriting Letters *L, l*: Words with *l*   **253**

Name _____

✏️ **Write**   🖍️ **Color**

_____
- - - - - - - - - - - - - - - - - -
_____

_____
- - - - - - - - - - - - - - - - - -
_____

_____
- - - - - - - - - - - - - - - - - -
_____

Ll

_____
- - - - - - - - - - - - - - - - - -
_____
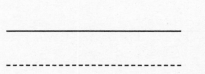

_____
- - - - - - - - - - - - - - - - - -
_____

_____
- - - - - - - - - - - - - - - - - -
_____

🍎 **Directions:** Name each picture. Write *l* on the line if the word begins with /l/. Color the /l/ pictures.

254 **Phonics** /l/ Spelled *Ll*

🏠 **Home Activity:** Have your child find pictures that begin with /l/ and paste the pictures on paper to make a /l/ book.

Lad can hop on the lid.

I can do that.

Are we on the lid?

4

Lad and Me

Lad is my cat.

Lad is little.

Do you like Lad?

1

Decodable Story *Lad and Me*
Target Skill /l/ Spelled *Ll*

I like Lad.

Lad can sit in my lap.

Lad can sit a lot.

Lad can hop.

Lad can hop a lot.

I can do that.

 **Write**  **Color**

do   that   are

_____

- - - - - - - - - - - - - - - - - - - -

_____ you see the man?

_____

Is _____ the lid?

_____

- - - - - - - - - - - - - - - - - - - -

We _____ at the top.

_____

- - - - - - - - - - - - - - - - - - - -

_____ you like my cat?

Directions: Read each sentence. Write the missing word to finish the sentence. Color the picture.

School + Home

Home Activity: Have your child use the high-frequency words in other sentences.

High-Frequency Words   **257**

Name _____

 Circle  Color

The cat ran.

The lad hops.

The rat hid.

Nan taps.

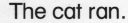 **Directions:** Circle the action part of the sentence and color the picture that shows the action. Use the action part in a sentence of your own.

 Home Activity: Help your child write simple sentences and identify the action part in each sentence.

Name _____

 Write  Color

_____
- -
id

_____
- -
hi

_____
- -
ap

L l

_____
- -
mi

_____
- -
ip

_____
- -
fi

 Directions: Write *l* if the word begins with /l/. Write *ll* if the word ends with /l/. Color the pictures.

 Home Activity: Have your child draw a picture of something that begins with /l/.

© Pearson Education, Inc., K

Phonics /l/ Spelled *Ll* **259**

Name _____

 **Draw**  **Color**

 Directions: Draw a line from what happened to why it happened. Color each picture.

School + Home **Home Activity:** Have your child tell why each event happened.

© Pearson Education, Inc., K

260 **Comprehension** Cause and Effect

Name _____

 **Circle**  **Color**

A cat ran fast.

Nan sits on it.

Tim hits the lid.

Lad can hop.

 Directions: Circle the naming part of the sentence. Then color the naming part of the picture. Then use the naming part in a sentence of your own.

 Home Activity: Have your child read each sentence and tell the naming part.

Conventions Naming Parts **261**

Name _____

✏️ Write   🖍️ Draw

_____

- -

_____

- -

_____

 Directions Have children copy the class poem they wrote about the fox. Then have them draw a picture of the fox.

 Home Activity Help your child make a poem with rhyming words such as *hit*, *bit*, *fit*, *kit*, and *sit*.

262 **Writing** Poem

Name _____

✏️ Draw

© Pearson Education, Inc., K

Directions: Draw a picture to show what happens next.

School + Home **Home Activity:** Ask your child to tell the beginning of the story and then tell about what happens next.

My Lucky Day

Comprehension Plot **263**

Name _____

My Lucky Day

 Circle  Write

 runs / sits

The dog _____.

 pets / hops

The frog _____.

 mop / hit

I _____.

 mops / pats

She _____ the cat.

 hit / sit

I _____ it.

 sits / taps

He _____ it.

Directions: Circle the action word to finish the sentence. Write the word on the lines.

 **Home Activity:** Have children read each sentence.

264 **Conventions** Action Parts

© Pearson Education, Inc., K

Name _____

✏️ **Write**

1 one

2 two

3 three

4 four

5 five

🍎 **Directions:** Write each number and number word on the lines.

 Home Activity: Ask your child to draw pictures to show each number.

Name _____

 Write 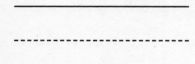Color

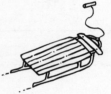

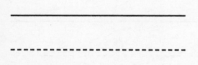

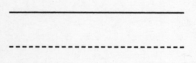

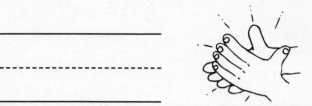

Directions: Name each picture. Write the blend for the beginning sound. Color the pictures.

Home Activity: Have your child point out initial consonant blends in the words in a book or magazine.

266 Phonics Consonant Blends *sl-, pl-, cl-, fl-*

I can tap.

Tap is like trap.

Do you see one trap?

Decodable Story *My Words*
Target Skill Consonant Blends

Name _____

My Words

I have one cap.

Cap is like clap.

Can you clap?

I see one cab.

Cab is like crab.

Can you see three?

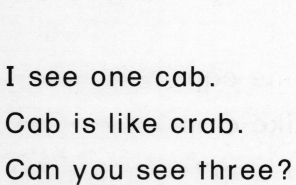

2

I can see one pot.

Pot is like spot.

Do you see two?

3

Name _____

 **Write**  **Color**

| one   two   three   four   five |

_____

I see _____ flags.

_____

I see _____ frogs.

_____

I see _____ rats.

_____

I see _____ clips.

Directions: Read each sentence. Write the missing word to finish the sentence. Color the picture .

 School + Home

Home Activity: Have your child use *one, two, three, four,* and *five* in other sentences.

Name _____

 Draw  Color

 Directions: Draw a line from the subject to the correct predicate. Color the pictures. Then use a complete sentence to tell what happens in each pair of pictures.

 Home Activity: Help your child write a complete sentence for each pair of pictures.

270 Conventions Complete Sentences

Name _____

 Write  Color

_____

ba

_____

ne

_____

mi

_____

ib

_____

ill

_____

ed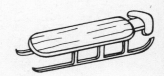

 © Pearson Education, Inc., K

Directions: Write the letters for the consonant blends to finish each word. Color the pictures.

 School +Home

Home Activity: Have your child use the words in sentences.

Name _____

 **Draw**  **Color**

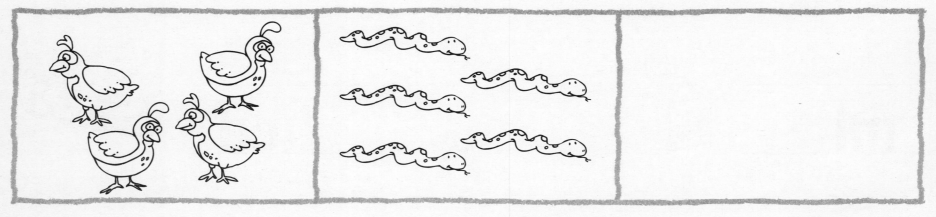

 Directions: Draw a picture to show which animal the mouse met next. Draw the right number of animals. Color the animals. Then tell what happened in order using words like *first*, *then next*, and *last*.

 Home Activity: Have your child draw pictures of the other animals the mouse met in the correct order.

Name _____

 Circle  Color

Tam ran to the spot.

Sam sits on the mat.

 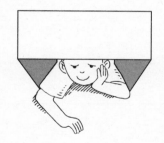

Bob hid in the top.

Lad hops to the cat.

 Directions Circle the action part of the sentence and color the picture that shows the action. Then use the action part in a sentence of your own.

 Home Activity Have your child tell about each picture and name the action part of each one.

© Pearson Education, Inc., K

Conventions Action Parts **273**

Name _____

✏️ **Draw**   ✏️ **Write**

_____
- -
_____

_____
- -
_____

Directions Draw a picture of the mouse in the story. Write or dictate a sentence that tells about the animal.

 School + Home **Home Activity** Have your child describe things about the mouse in the story.

Name _____

  **Circle** **Color**

She is _____ .

mad

sad

She is _____ .

mad

sad

 Directions: Circle the word to finish the sentence. Color the pictures.

School + Home **Home Activity:** Have your child tell why he or she drew the conclusion he or she did.

© Pearson Education, Inc., K

Comprehension Draw Conclusions **275**

Name _____

 **Draw**

One cat had

to the flag.

Two dogs ran

a hat.

Three rats sat

a big pot.

Four pigs see

on a mat.

 Directions Draw a line to the words that complete each sentence.

 Home Activity Help your child tell about the picture and read the sentences.

Name _____

Write

_____

- -

_____

_____

- -

_____

_____   _____

- - - - - - - - - - - - - - -   - - - - - - - - - - - - - - -

Gil _____   got _____

Directions Have children write a row of each letter and then write the words.

Home Activity Ask your child to show you how to write each letter.

Name _____

 **Write**    **Color**

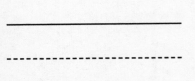

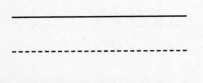
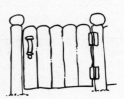

Gg

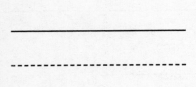

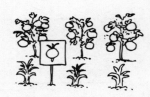

 Directions: Name each picture. Write *g* on the line if the word begins with /g/. Color the /g/ pictures.

 Home Activity: Have your child find pictures that begin with /g/ and paste the pictures on paper to make a /g/ book.

How Many?

Lin and Hap can see
one dog.

Can you see four frogs?

Lin and Hap can see
five frogs.

Decodable Story *How Many?*
Target Skill /g/ Spelled *Gg*

Lin and Hap can see
two kids.

Lin and Hap can see
three pigs.

2

3

Name _____

 Write  Color

| one | two | three | four | five |

_____

- - - - - - - - - - - - - - - - -

I can see _____.

_____

- - - - - - - - - - - - - - - - -

I can see _____.

_____

- - - - - - - - - - - - - - - - -

I can see _____.

_____

- - - - - - - - - - - - - - - - -

I can see _____.

 Directions: Read each sentence. Write the missing word to finish the sentence. Color the picture.

School + Home **Home Activity:** Have your child use the number words in sentences to tell about things in your home.

High-Frequency Words **281**

Name _____

 Draw  Color

| The dog can nab it. | The pig is big. | The cat had one hat. | The log is little. |

 Directions: Draw a line from the sentence to the picture it tells about. Then point to and tell about the naming and action parts of the sentence shown in the picture. Color the pictures.

 Home Activity: Ask your child to make another statement that tells about each picture.

282 **Conventions** Telling Sentences

Name _____

 Write  Color

oat **do** **be** **ate**

le **ap** **um** **pi**

 Directions: Write the letter to finish each word. Color the pictures that begin or end with /g/.

 Home Activity: Have your child name the pictures that begin with /g/.

Phonics /g/ Spelled Gg   **283**

Name _____

 Color

Directions: Look at the top picture. Color the characters from *Goldilocks and the Three Bears* in the boxes.

 Home Activity: Have your child tell about what is happening in the top picture.

284 **Comprehension** Characters

Name _____

 **Draw**

 A frog sat   to dig.

 The pigs like   on a log.

 Gil has   the top.

Nan likes   a big hat.

 Directions Draw a line to the words that complete each sentence.

 Home Activity Help your child tell about the picture and read the sentences.

Conventions Complete Sentences   **285**

Name _____

✏️ Write

1. ------------------------

2. ------------------------

3. ------------------------

 Directions Write or dictate a list of things found in the story.

286 **Writing** List

 School + Home **Home Activity** Help your child write a list. It could be a job list or list of things to do.

© Pearson Education, Inc., K

Name _____

✏️ Draw   🖍️ Color

Directions: Tell a story about the first box. Then draw the setting in the box.

School + Home

Home Activity: Have your child tell you about the setting for each story.

Comprehension Setting   **287**

© Pearson Education, Inc., K

Name _____

 Color  Draw

| Gil naps on the mat. | The cat had a cap. | Tad had the top. | Nan had a tan rat. |

 Directions: Draw a line from the sentence to the picture it tells about. Color the pictures, then tell another sentence about each picture.

 Home Activity: Have your child create sentences about people he or she knows.

Name _____

 **Write**

_____

- -

_____

- -

_____

_____   _____

Ed - - - - - - - - - - - - - - -   **egg** - - - - - - - - - - - - - - -
_____   _____

 Directions Have children write a row of each letter and then write the words.

 School + Home **Home Activity** Ask your child to show you how to write each letter.

Handwriting Letters *E, e:* Words with *e*   **289**

Name _____

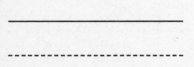 Write   Color

_____

_____

_____

Ee

_____

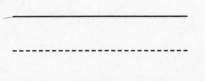

_____

_____

 Directions: Name each picture. Write *e* on the line if the word begins with /e/. Color the /e/ pictures.

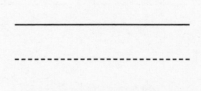 **Home Activity:** Look through a newspaper or book with your child and point out words that begin with /e/.

290   **Phonics** /e/ Spelled *Ee*

ten hens

ten bells

ten pens

I see ten, ten, ten!

4

Decodable Story *Ten, Ten, Ten!*
Target Skill /e/ Spelled *Ee*

Ten, Ten, Ten!

I have a pet hen.

Do you see my hen?

I can see ten.

1

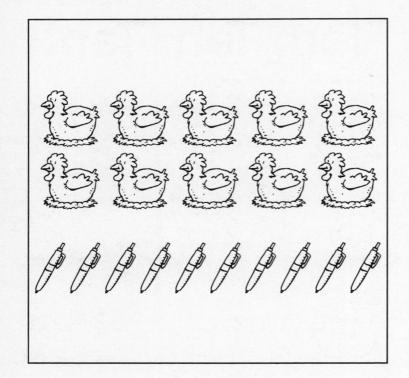

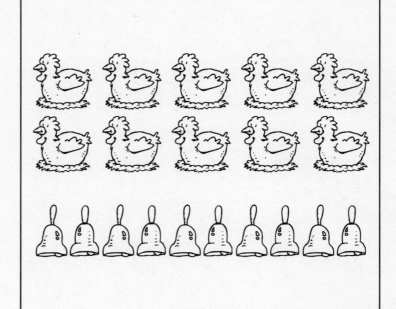

I have a fat pen.

Do you see my pen?

I can see ten.

2

I have a red bell.

Do you see my bell?

I can see ten.

3

Name _____

 **Write**  **Color**

here   go   from

_____

- -

Go _____ here to here.

_____

- -

You can go _____.

_____

- -

We can _____ fast.

_____

- -

It is _____ me.

Directions: Read each sentence. Write the missing word to finish the sentence. Color the picture.

Home Activity: Have your child use the high-frequency words in other sentences.

© Pearson Education, Inc., K

Name _____

 Write  Draw

the pet sat in a tent

_____

- -

_____

© Pearson Education, Inc., K

Directions: Write the sentence using an uppercase letter and a period. Draw a picture for the sentence.

 School + Home

Home Activity: Write sentences without uppercase letters and periods. Have your child write the sentences correctly.

294 **Conventions** Uppercase Letters and Periods

Name _____

 Write   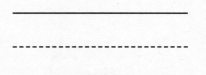 **Color**

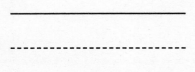

 **Ee**

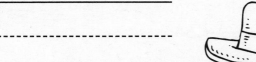

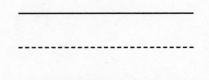

 Directions: Name each picture. Write the letter for the middle sound of each picture. Color the /e/ pictures.

 Home Activity: Help your child make a list of words with /e/.

Phonics /e/ Spelled *Ee*   **295**

© Pearson Education, Inc., K

Name _____

 Circle  Color

© Pearson Education, Inc., K

Directions: Circle things that belong together. Color those pictures in each row.

School + Home **Home Activity:** Have your child draw three things that belong to the same group—toys, foods, or clothes.

296 **Comprehension** Classify and Categorize

Name _____

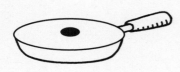 **Draw**

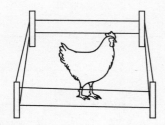   The lid is   on the bed.

   One hen sat   on the pan.

   The net is   a big cat.

   The pet is   in the pen.

 Directions Draw a line to the words that complete each sentence.

School + Home **Home Activity** Help your child tell about the picture and read the sentences.

Conventions Telling Sentences   **297**

© Pearson Education, Inc., K

Name _____

 Write

_____

- -

Dear _____ ,

_____

- -

I like to read about _____

_____

- -

_____

Your friend,

_____

- -

_____

© Pearson Education, Inc., K

Directions Write or dictate a letter to someone. Finish the sentence that tells what you like to read about and then write your name.

 Home Activity Help your child write a letter to a family member or friend.

298 **Writing** Informal Letter

Name _____

 Draw

Directions: Draw your own picture to show what
If You Could Go to Antartica is all about.

 Home Activity: Have your child tell about his or her
picture.

Comprehension Main Idea **299**

Name _____

 Write 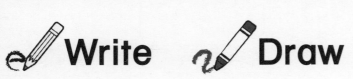 Draw

my pet has a net

Directions: Write the sentence using an uppercase letter and a period. Draw a picture for the sentence.

 Home Activity: Point to and read sentences in a book and have your child identify the uppercase letter and the period. Ask your child to copy one of the sentences.

Name _____

 Write

_____

- -

_____

_____

- -

_____

bed _____

net _____

hen _____

pet _____

 Directions: Have children write a row of each letter and then write the words.

 Home Activity: Ask your child to show you how to write each letter.

Name _____

 Write    Color

h ___ n

b ___ d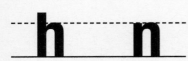

h ___ t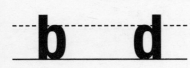

Ee

m ___ p

p ___ n

n ___ t

 Directions: Write *e, a,* or *o* to finish each word. Color the /e/ pictures.

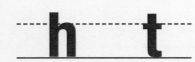 **Home Activity:** Have your child write *pen* and *pan* and draw a picture for each word.

You can see the tent.

You can see the nest.

I have a pet.

© Pearson Education, Inc., K

Decodable Story *Ted and the Pet*
Target Skill /e/ Spelled *Ee*

Ted and the Pet

I am Ted.

I have a pet.

My pet is big.

I met my pet here.

My pet is in the tent.

It is a big tent.

My pet can go to the tent.

My pet has a nest in the tent.

It is a big nest.

Name _____

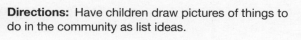 Draw

 Directions: Have children draw pictures of things to do in the community as list ideas.

 Home Activity: Ask your child to tell you about his or her pictures of things to do in the community.

Name _____

 **Draw**  **Write**

Directions Have children illustrate the class list topic and dictate or write a question about the topic.

Home Activity Ask your child to tell you about the list the class is planning to write.

306 **Writing Process** Planning

 Write  Color

here   go   from

_____

- -

Did you _____ here?

_____

- -

I did not go _____.

_____

- -

I had to go _____ here to here.

_____

- -

I will _____ here.

© Pearson Education, Inc., K

Directions: Read each sentence. Write the missing word to finish the sentence. Color the picture.

Home Activity: Have your child use the high-frequency words in other sentences.

Name _____

 Read It!

I have a pet dog.

The pet is for me.

Say It!

Tell about something you have using the words **I** and **me**.

 **Write It!**

_____

_____have a book. (I)

_____

The book is for _____. (me)

 Directions Have children read the sentences with you. Ask them to give sentences for things they have using *I* and *me*. Then have children write the words *I* and *me* to complete the sentences.

 Home Activity Have your child read the sentences and find the pronouns *I* and *me*. Then have him or her create sentences with the pronouns *I* and *me*.

© Pearson Education, Inc., K

Circle

REFERENCE

Directions: Ask: Which sources would you use to find out about tomorrow's weather in our community? Have children circle the best source(s) for that information and then tell why.

School + Home

Home Activity: Discuss with your child ways that TV can be a good source of information.

Name _____

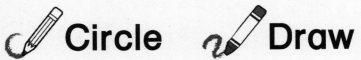 Circle  Draw

☆ DAILY STAR ☆
Tallahassee and Ft. Worth win recycling awards.

Directions: Ask: Which source or sources would you use to find something new to do in our community? Have children circle the best source(s) for that information. In the empty space have them draw another source they could use to answer the question. Discuss their choices.

 Home Activity: Suggest various types of information and have your child tell where to look for the information.

310 **Writing Process** Sources

Circle  **Color**

bed bad		bet bat	
log leg		pen pan	

Directions: Circle the word that names the picture. Color the /e/ pictures.

 Home Activity: Have your child draw a picture of something with /e/.

Name _____

 Draw  Color

 Directions: Draw a picture in the last box that tells where the story happened. Color the pictures.

 Home Activity: Draw a picture of where and when one of your favorite stories happened.

Name _____

 Write  Draw

the hen likes the pen

_____

- -

_____

 Directions: Write the sentence using an uppercase letter and a period. Draw a picture for the sentence.

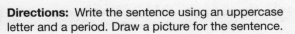 **Home Activity:** Point to and read sentences in a book. Have your child identify the uppercase letter and the period. Then help your child create several sentences.

Conventions Uppercase Letters and Periods **313**

Name _____

 Write  Draw

1. _____
_____

2. _____
_____

3. _____
_____

 Directions Have children write, dictate, or copy their draft or key words from the class list. Have them draw pictures for the words in your list.

 Home Activity Ask your child to tell you what he or she learned about the topic of the class list.

Name _____

🖍 **Color**

🍎 **Directions:** Color the pictures that show something real.

School + Home **Home Activity:** Have your child draw a picture of a real ocean.

Comprehension Realism and Fantasy   **315**

Name _____

Abuela

 Read It!

I have a cat.

The cat is for me.

Say It!

Tell about something you have using the words **I** and **me**.

 **Write It!**

_____

- - - - - - - - - - - - - - - -

_____have a pet. (I)

_____

- - - - - - - - - - - - - - -

The pet is for _____. (me)

 Directions Have children read the sentences with you. Ask them to give sentences for things they have using *I* and *me*. Then have children write the words *I* and *me* to complete the sentences.

 **Home Activity** Have your child read the sentences and find the pronouns *I* and *me*. Then have him or her create sentences with the pronouns *I* and *me*.

316 **Conventions** Pronouns *I* and *Me*

Abuela

Name _____

 Write 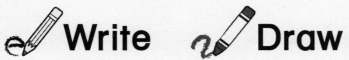 Draw

I will add this to my draft.

_____

- -

_____

_____

- -

_____

 Directions Have children draw pictures of and write or dictate additional information that could be included in the class list.

 Home Activity Have your child tell you how the class revised the list to make it better.

Name _____

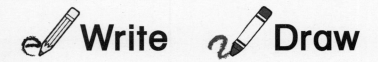 Write 　 Draw

_____

- -

_____

- -

_____

- -

_____

© Pearson Education, Inc., K

 Directions Have children draw, write, or dictate the entire class list.

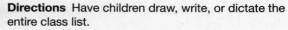 **Home Activity** Discuss with your child another topic he or she would like to write about. Try drafting a list on this topic.

Name _____

 Circle  Write

1. you cango swimming in Lake Michigan.

----

2. you can see animals at twobig zoos.

----

3. you can eat deep-dishpizza.

 Directions Read the sentences together. Help children find the errors. Have them circle the mistakes and rewrite the words or sentences correctly on the lines.

 Home Activity Have your child point out and explain his or her edits.

Name _____

 Circle  Write

_____

I shared my selection with _____.

Here's what he/she learned.

_____

_____

_____

 Directions Have children circle the picture that shows with whom they shared their list. Then have children ask the peer or adult reviewer to fill in the blanks and to discuss the list with him or her.

 Home Activity Ask your child to read or tell the class list to you.

320 Writing Process Sharing

Name _____

 Write

J _____

j _____

W _____

w _____

Jen _____

Will _____

Directions Have children write a row of each letter and then write the words.

School + Home **Home Activity** Ask your child to write each letter and tell you how to make the letter.

Handwriting Letters *Jj, Ww:* Words with *j, w* **321**

Name _____

 Write  Color

Jj
Ww

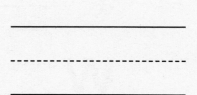

 Directions: Name each picture. Write *j* if the word begins with /j/. Write *w* if the word begins with /w/. Color the /j/ pictures.

School + Home **Home Activity:** Have your child find other words with /j/ or /w/.

You can get on the big, blue jet.

You can go with Jen and Will.

4

Decodable Story *Jen and Will*
Target Skill /j/ Spelled *Jj*, /w/ Spelled *Ww*

Jen and Will

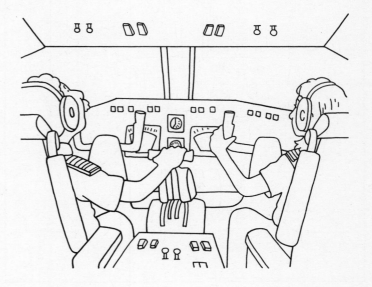

Jen and Will get on the jet.

It is a big, blue jet.

1

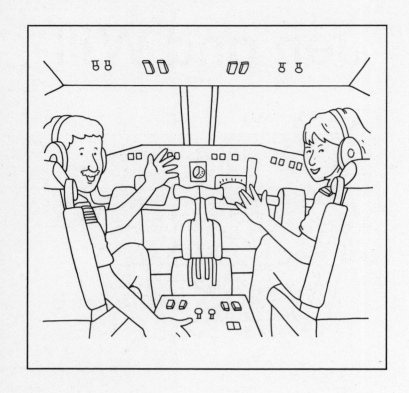

Jen and Will have jobs
on the jet.

Jen and Will like the jobs.

Jen and Will get the jet
to go.

They can see you.

Name _____

 Write  Color

yellow   blue   green   have

_____

- -

The pond is _____.

_____

- -

Is the sun _____?

_____

- -

My top is _____.

_____

- -

I _____ a cat.

Directions: Read each sentence. Write the missing word to finish the sentence and color the picture.

Home Activity: Have your child use the high-frequency words in other sentences.

High-Frequency Words   325

Name _____

 Draw

Can you jog?

Do you like to skip?

Can you hop?

Can you get the bell?

 I like to skip.

 I can jog.

I can get the bell.

I can not hop.

 Directions: Draw a line from each question to its answer.

 Home Activity: Ask your child the questions and have him or her create an answer.

326 **Conventions** Questions

© Pearson Education, Inc., K

Name _____

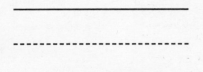 Write    Color

_____
- - - - - - - - - - - - - - - - - -
_____

_____
- - - - - - - - - - - - - - - - - -
_____

_____
- - - - - - - - - - - - - - - - - -
_____

Jj
Ww

_____
- - - - - - - - - - - - - - - - - -
_____

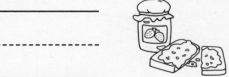

_____
- - - - - - - - - - - - - - - - - -
_____

_____
- - - - - - - - - - - - - - - - - -
_____

 Directions: Name each picture and spell the picture name. Write the word on the lines. Then color the /j/ and /w/ pictures.

 Home Activity: Have your child draw pictures of things that begin with /j/ and /w/.

Phonics /j/ Spelled *Jj*, /w/ Spelled *Ww*   **327**

Name _____

 **Write**

 Directions: Label the animal in each picture *R* for real or *M* for make-believe.

 Home Activity: Have your child draw and color a picture of a real animal and where it lives.

328 **Comprehension** Realism and Fantasy

Name _____

Read It!

I have a box.

The box is for me.

Say It!

Tell about something you have using the words **I** and **me**.

Write It!

_____

- - - - - - - - - - - - - - - - - - - -

_____ have a bat. (I)

_____

- - - - - - - - - - - - - - - - - - - -

The bat is for _____. (me)

 Directions Have children track the print and read the sentences with you. Ask children to say sentences for things they have using *I* and *me*. Then have children write the pronouns *I* and *me* to complete the sentences.

 Home Activity Have your child read the sentences and find the pronouns *I* and *me*. Then have him or her create sentences with the pronouns *I* and *me*.

© Pearson Education, Inc., K

Name _____

 Draw 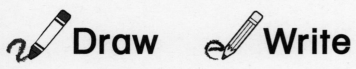 Write

 Directions Have children draw a picture of an animal home. Have them use content-based vocabulary, such as social studies words, to write or dictate a caption for their picture.

 Home Activity Show pictures and have your child think of a caption for each picture.

330 **Writing** Caption

Name _____

© Pearson Education, Inc., K

✏️ **Number**

 Directions Write the numbers 1, 2, and 3 to tell what happened at the beginning, in the middle, and near the end of *Max Takes the Train*.

 Home Activity Have your child tell the story using the pictures.

Comprehension Plot   **331**

Name _____

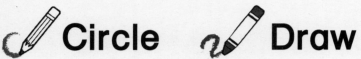 Circle  Draw

Where is the fan?
The fan is by the mat.

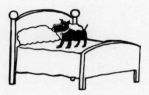

The dog is on the big bed.
What is big?

Where is the book?
Jen set the book on the box.

Then hen is in the pen.
Where is the hen?

© Pearson Education, Inc., K

 Directions: Read the sentences. Circle the question.
Then draw a line under the answer to the question.

School + Home **Home Activity:** Ask your child to read each question
and answer. Then have him or her give other questions
about the pictures.

332 Conventions Questions

Name _____

 **Write**

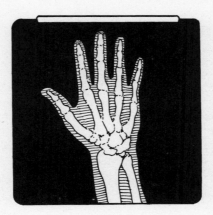

_____

- -

_____

_____

- -

_____

six _____

box _____

Directions: Have children write a row of each letter
and then write the words.

 Home Activity: Ask your child to show you how to
write each letter.

Handwriting Letters *X, x:* Words with *x* **333**

Name _____

 Write    Color

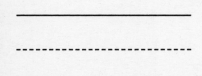

_____
- -
_____

_____
- -
_____

_____
- -
_____

 Xx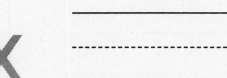

6

_____
- -
_____

_____
- -
_____

© Pearson Education, Inc., K

Directions: Name each picture. Write *x* on the line if the word ends with /ks/. Color the /ks/ pictures.

School + Home **Home Activity:** Help your child find pictures or words that end with /ks/ to make a /ks/ booklet.

Max can see his pal Rex.

Max and Rex can mix yellow and red.

Decodable Story *Max*
Target Skill /ks/ Spelled *Xx*

Name _____

Max

Max is six.

He hid in a box.

He hid from his mom.

Max can look like a fox.

He has four legs.

2

Max can mix blue and green.

It is an ox.

3

Name _____

 **Write**    **Color**

| green   blue   yellow   for |

_____

- - - - - - - - - - - - - - - - - - - -

My dog is _____ .

_____

- - - - - - - - - - - - - - - - - - - -

The hill is _____ .

_____

- - - - - - - - - - - - - - - - - - - -

I have a cat _____ you.

_____

- - - - - - - - - - - - - - - - - - - -

I like that _____ hat.

 Directions: Read each sentence. Write the missing word to finish the sentence. Color the picture.

 **Home Activity:** Have your child use the high-frequency words in other sentences.

High-Frequency Words   337

© Pearson Education, Inc., K

Name _____

 Write 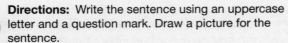 **Draw**

can I get a pet

_____

- -

_____

Directions: Write the sentence using an uppercase letter and a question mark. Draw a picture for the sentence.

 School + Home

Home Activity: Write other questions without uppercase letters and question marks. Have your child write the questions correctly.

338 **Conventions** Question Marks and Uppercase Letters

Name _____

 Write   Color

_____
- - - - - - - - - - - -
_____

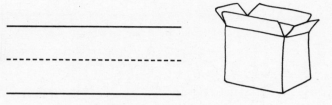

_____
- - - - - - - - - - - -
_____

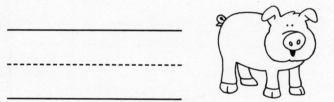

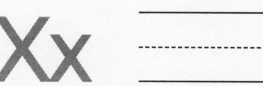 Xx

_____
- - - - - - - - - - - -
_____

_____
- - - - - - - - - - - -
_____

6

_____
- - - - - - - - - - - -
_____

_____
- - - - - - - - - - - -
_____

 Directions: Name each picture and spell the picture name. Write the word on the lines. Then color the pictures that end with /ks/.

 Home Activity: Have your child draw a picture of something that ends with /ks/.

Phonics /ks/ Spelled *Xx* **339**

Name _____

 Draw  Color

 Directions: Draw a line from what happened to why it happened. Color each picture.

 Home Activity: Have your child tell you what happened in each picture and why it happened.

© Pearson Education, Inc., K

 **Circle**  **Color**

I see a cat.

Do you see a cat?

Do you see Nan?

I see Nan.

What can Tim hit?

Tim hits the lid.

Lad can hop.

What can Lad do?

 Directions: Circle the question. Underline the answer. Then color the pictures.

 Home Activity: Have your child read each question and answer. Then help them say and write other questions and answers.

Name _____

✏️ Write   🖍️ Draw

_____
- -
_____
_____
- -
_____

 Directions Have children copy the rhyme about saving the boat. Then have them draw a picture of it.

School + Home **Home Activity** Help your child make a poem with rhyming words such as *boat, goat, coal,* and *float.*

Name _____

✏️ **Write**

Directions: Number the boxes to show what happens first, next, and last in each story. Then retell the story using the words *first, next,* and *last.*

 Home Activity: Ask your child to draw three pictures that show how to make a sandwich.

Comprehension Sequence   **343**

Name _____

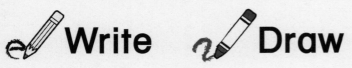 Write Draw

where can I get a pet

_____

- -

_____

© Pearson Education, Inc., K

Directions: Write the sentence using an uppercase letter and a question mark. Draw a picture for the sentence.

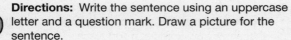 **Home Activity:** Choose a variety of topics and help your child create questions and answers about the topic.

Name _____

✏️ Write

_____

- -

_____

_____

- -

_____

Ula - - - - - - - - - - - - - - - -

up - - - - - - - - - - - - - - - -

🍎 **Directions:** Have children write a row of each letter and then write the words.

 Home Activity: Ask your child to show you how to write each letter.

Handwriting Letters *U, u:* Words with *u*   **345**

Name _____

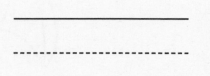 Write  Color

Uu

 Directions: Name each picture. Write *u* on the line if the word begins with /u/. Color the /u/ pictures.

School + Home **Home Activity:** Look through a newspaper or book with your child and point out words that begin with /u/.

346 **Phonics** /u/ Spelled *Uu*

Jud ran to his pals.

Jud said, "Let us go in!

We will have fun!"

Fun for Jud

The sun was hot.

Jud got up from bed.

Jud has to have a plan.

What can he do for fun?

Jud will see his pals.

What will they do for fun?

Name _____

  **Write** **Color**

| what | was | said | she |

_____

_____ she with you?

_____

_____ is my mom.

_____

He _____ she was with me.

_____

_____ did you see?

 Directions: Read each sentence. Write the missing word to finish the sentence. Color the picture.

 **Home Activity:** Have your child use the high-frequency words in other sentences.

High-Frequency Words 349

Name _____

 Read It!

The pet is on the box.

Say It!

Say a sentence about a cat

using the word **in**.

 **Write It!**

 **by the book**

_____

- - - - - - - - - - - - - - - - - - -

The dog sat _____ the book.

 Directions Have children track the print and read the sentence with you. Ask them to say a sentence about a cat with the word *in*. Then have children write the preposition *by* to complete the sentence.

 Home Activity Have your child create sentences using the prepositions *on*, *in*, or *by*.

© Pearson Education, Inc., K

Name _____

 Write  Color

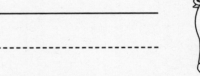

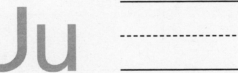

Uu

 Directions: Name each picture and spell the picture name. Write the word on the lines. Then color the /u/ pictures.

 Home Activity: Help your child make a list of words with /u/.

Name _____

Color

 Directions: Color each matching pair a different color.

 Home Activity: Have your child compare and contrast the bike messengers by telling how the pictures are alike and how they are different.

352 **Comprehension** Compare and Contrast

Name _____

 Write  Draw

can I see the pet

_____

- -

_____

 Directions: Write the question using an uppercase letter and a question mark. Draw a picture for the sentence.

 Home Activity: Write a short question on paper and read the question. Have your child identify the uppercase letter and the question mark. Then help your child create and write another question.

Conventions Question Marks and Uppercase Letters **353**

Name _____

✏️ Write 🖍️ Draw

_____

- -

_____

- -

_____

 Directions Have children copy the poem about the truck. Then have them draw a picture of the truck.

 Home Activity Help your child make a poem with rhyming words such as *truck, luck, stuck,* and *duck.*

Name _____

 Circle  Color

 Directions: Circle the picture that shows what you think will happen next. Color the pictures.

 School + Home **Home Activity:** Have your child explain how he or she arrived at each conclusion.

Comprehension Draw Conclusions **355**

Name _____

 **Read It!**

The bug sat on the rug.

Say It!

Use **by** in a sentence about something in the room.

 **Write It!**

_____

The bug sat _____ the tub. (in)

 Directions Have children track the print and read the sentence with you. Ask them to say a sentence about something in the room using *by*. Then have children write the preposition *in* to complete the sentence.

 Home Activity Point to things and have your child tell where they are, using the prepositions *on, in, near,* or *by*—near the table, on the couch, by the door.

© Pearson Education, Inc., K

Name _____

Write

_____

- -

_____

- -

_____

cup _____

bus _____

nut _____

bug _____

Directions: Have children write a row of each letter and then write the words.

School + Home **Home Activity:** Ask your child to show you how to write each letter.

Name _____

 Write  Color

c __ t

b __ s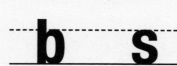

t __ b

 Uu

p __ n

t __ p

n __ t

 Directions: Write *i*, *o*, or *u* to finish each word. Color the /u/ pictures.

 Home Activity: Have your child write *rug* and *bug* and draw a picture for each word.

Jan and Gus are on
the rug.

Jan and Gus are pals.

4

Decodable Story *Jan and Gus*
Target Skill /u/ Spelled *Uu*

Jan and Gus

Jan and Gus are pals.

They like to have fun.

1

Jan and Gus like the sun.

They like to hum on the bus.

Jan and Gus see a bug.

They run in the mud.

Name _____

 Write  Color

what   am   said   was

_____

I _____ five.

_____

I _____ four.

_____

_____ can I do?

_____

I _____ I can help.

Directions: Read each sentence. Write the missing word to finish the sentence. Color the picture.

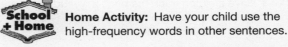 **Home Activity:** Have your child use the high-frequency words in other sentences.

Name _____

 **Read It!**

The bus is big.

Say It!

Use the word **sun** in

a sentence.

 **Write It!**

_____

The _____ is big. (bug)

 Directions Have children track the print and read the sentence with you. Ask them to say a sentence about the sun. Then have children write the noun to complete the sentence.

 Home Activity: Have your child use the nouns *bus, sun,* and *bug* in other sentences.

362 **Conventions** Nouns

Name _____

 Write  Color

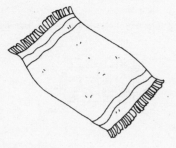

_____

- -

_____

_____

- -

_____

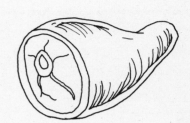

_____

- -

_____

_____

- -

_____

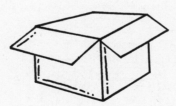

_____

- -

_____

_____

- -

_____

Directions: Say the word that names the picture. Spell the picture name. Write the word on the lines. Color the /u/ pictures.

 Home Activity: Have your child draw a picture of something with /u/.

Phonics /u/ Spelled *Uu*   **363**

Name _____

 Color

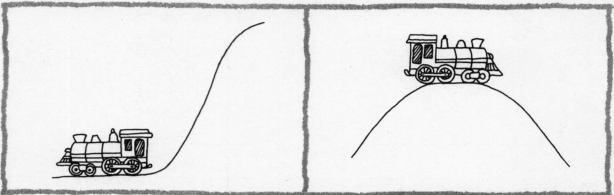

 Directions: Color the picture that shows what would happen next in each story.

 Home Activity: Have your child tell what he or she does after putting on his or her pajamas.

364 Comprehension Plot

Name _____

 **Read It!**

The dog is under the table.

Say It!

Use the word **on** in a sentence about something in the classroom.

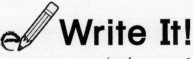 **Write It!**

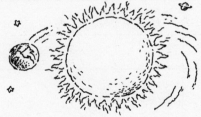

_____

- - - - - - - - - - - - - - - -

The sun is _____ the sky. (in)

 Directions Have children track the print and read the sentence about the dog. Ask them to say a sentence using the word *on*. Then have children write the preposition to complete the sentence about the sun.

 Home Activity Have your child use the prepositions *on, in,* or *under* in sentences. Provide sentence clues as needed.

© Pearson Education, Inc., K

Name _____

✏️ Write

_____

- -

Dear _____ ,

_____

- -

_____

_____

- -

_____

Your friend,

_____

- -

_____

 Directions Have children compose a letter to someone. Have them write or dictate the person's name and a sentence that tells about a toy they like. Then have children write their name.

 Home Activity Help your child write a letter to a family member or friend.

Name _____

 **Color**  **Draw**

 Directions: Color the pictures. Then draw a picture in the last box that shows who the character in each story is.

 School + Home **Home Activity:** Have your child draw a picture of the characters in one of his or her favorite stories.

Name _____

 **Read It!**

The mug is big.

Say It!

Tell something about the bug. Use the word **bug** in your sentence.

 **Write It!**

_____

- -

The _____ is big. (sun)

 Directions Have children track the print and read the sentence about the mug. Ask them to tell something about a bug. Then have children write the noun to complete the sentence.

 Home Activity Have your child give another sentence about each picture.

Name _____

 Write

V ------------------------------------

v ------------------------------------

Z ------------------------------------

z ------------------------------------

Viv ------------------------------------

zip ------------------------------------

Directions Have children write a row of each letter and then write the words.

 Home Activity Ask your child to show how you write each letter.

Handwriting Letters *Vv, Zz*: Words with *v, z* **369**

Name _____

 Write    **Color**

Vv
Zz

 Directions: Name each picture. Write *v* if the word begins with /v/. Write *z* if the word begins with /z/. Color the /v/ pictures.

 Home Activity: Have your child find other words that begin with /v/ or /z/.

He will zap the tag.

Val has got the red top.

Decodable Story *Val's Top*
Target Skill /v/ Spelled *Vv*, /z/ Spelled *Zz*

Val's Top

Val and Mom come in a van.

They will go to look for a top.

Val and Mom see a top.

They can zip it up.

The top is red.

Val and Mom like the top.

Name _____

 Write  Color

where   is   come   me

_____

Do they see _____?

_____

_____ did you go?

_____

_____ here, little dog.

_____

My mom _____ here.

Directions: Read each sentence. Write the missing word to finish the sentence. Color the picture.

School + Home **Home Activity:** Have your child use the high-frequency words in other sentences.

Name _____

 Circle  Write

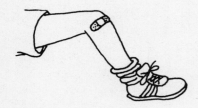

leg

run

_____

- - - - - - - - - - - - - - -

My _____ got cut.

sit

pal

_____

- - - - - - - - - - - - -

This is my _____.

pig

big

_____

- - - - - - - - - - - - -

Come here, little _____.

hop

bug

_____

- - - - - - - - - - - - -

Look at the _____.

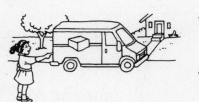

van

will

_____

- - - - - - - - - - - - -

That _____ is big.

hit

hill

_____

- - - - - - - - - - - - -

Run up the _____.

 Directions: Circle the noun that matches the picture. Write the word to complete the sentence.

School + Home **Home Activity:** Have your child read each sentence.

© Pearson Education, Inc., K

374 **Conventions** Nouns in Sentences

Name _____

  Write Color

_____
- - - - - - - - - - - - - - - -
_____

6

_____
- - - - - - - - - - - - - - - -
_____

_____
- - - - - - - - - - - - - - - -
_____

Vv
Zz

_____
- - - - - - - - - - - - - - - -
_____

_____
- - - - - - - - - - - - - - - -
_____

_____
- - - - - - - - - - - - - - - -
_____

 Directions: Name each picture and spell the picture name. Write the word on the lines. Then color the /z/ and /v/ pictures.

School + Home **Home Activity:** Have your child draw pictures of things that begin with /v/ and /z/.

Phonics /v/ Spelled *Vv*, /z/ Spelled *Zz* **375**

Name _____

✏️ **Color**

 Directions: Color the picture that shows the main idea of the story *On the Move!*

 Home Activity: Have your child tell you about the story and why he or she chose the main idea picture. Also have your child tell why the other pictures do not show the main idea.

Name _____

On the Move!

Read It!

The cub is little.

Say It!

Tell something about the tub. Use the word **tub** in your sentence.

Write It!

_____

- - - - - - - - - - - - - - - -

The _____ is little. (nut)

 Directions Have children read the sentence about the cub. Ask them to say a sentence about the tub. Then have children write the noun to complete the sentence.

 Home Activity Point to items in the house and have your child name the item and use the word in a sentence.

© Pearson Education, Inc., K

Conventions Nouns **377**

Name _____

 Draw  **Write**

Come to our play.

_____

- -

It is on _____.
_____

- - - - - - - - - - - - -

It is at _____ o'clock.

 Directions Draw a picture for your class play. Then write or dictate the missing information for the class.

 Home Activity Help your child create an invitation to a real or make believe family event.

Name _____

 Draw  Color

 Directions: Draw a line from what happened to why it happened. Color each picture.

 Home Activity: Have your child tell why each event happened.

Comprehension Cause and Effect   **379**

Name _____

 Circle **Write**

 cup

pup

_____

- - - - - - - - - -

The little _____ is here.

 cat

rat

_____

- - - - - - - - - -

The little _____ ran.

 hen

pen

_____

- - - - - - - - - -

One fat _____ is here.

 log

dog

_____

- - - - - - - - - -

The _____ likes it.

 pet

net

_____

- - - - - - - - - -

The little _____ is wet.

 fan

man

_____

- - - - - - - - - -

A cat ran to the _____ .

© Pearson Education, Inc., K

 Directions: Look at the picture. Read the sentence. Circle the noun to complete the sentence. Write the word.

School + Home **Home Activity:** Have your child use the noun that is not circled in each box in a sentence.

380 **Conventions** Nouns in Sentences

Name _____

✏️ **Write**

Y

y

Q

q

yet _____

Quin _____

🍎 **Directions** Have children write a row of each letter
and then write the words.

 Home Activity Ask your child to write each letter and tell
you how to make the letter.

Handwriting Letters *Yy*, *Qq*: Words with *y*, *q*   **381**

Name _____

 Write    **Color**

**Yy
Qq**

 Directions: Name each picture. Write *y* if the word begins with /y/. Write *qu* if the word begins with /kw/. Color the /kw/ pictures.

School + Home **Home Activity:** Have your child find other words with /y/ or /kw/.

Tim ran to the end.

Tim had a rest.

Decodable Story *Run, Tim*
Target Skill /y/ Spelled *Yy*, /kw/ Spelled *Qq*

Run, Tim

Tim ran past his sis.

She said,

"You can not quit yet."

Tim ran up a hill.

His dad said,

"You can not quit yet."

2

Tim ran and ran.

His mom said,

"You can not quit yet."

3

Name _____

✎ **Draw**

 Directions Have children draw pictures of
themselves doing or making things as topic ideas for
the how-to report.

 Home Activity Ask your child to tell you about his or her
pictures of topic ideas.

Name _____

 Draw  Write

© Pearson Education, Inc., K

🍎 **Directions** Have children illustrate or write the class
how-to report topic question and dictate or write
another question about the topic.

 Home Activity Ask your child to tell you about the
how-to report the class is planning to write.

386 **Writing** Process Planning

Name _____

 Write  Color

| come   we   where   she |

_____

- -

_____ can see me.

_____

- -

_____ will you go?

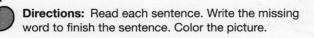

_____

- -

_____ can run fast.

_____

- -

_____ and see this bug.

 Directions: Read each sentence. Write the missing word to finish the sentence. Color the picture.

School + Home **Home Activity:** Have your child use the high-frequency words in other sentences.

Name _____

 Circle   **Write**

   dog

sat

_____

- - - - - - - - - - - - - - -

She _____ on the bus.

     look

yet

_____

- - - - - - - - - - - - - - -

We _____ up at a jet.

    hat

ran

_____

- - - - - - - - - - - - - - -

My dog _____ to me.

   see

bag

_____

- - - - - - - - - - - - - - -

_____ my cat!

   hop

leg

_____

- - - - - - - - - - - - - - -

He can _____ .

   bell

sit

_____

- - - - - - - - - - - - - - -

Can I _____ here?

 Directions: Circle the verb that matches the picture.
Write the word to complete the sentence.

 Home Activity: Have your child read each sentence.

Name _____

 Circle

☆ DAILY STAR ☆
Tallahassee and Ft. Worth win recycling awards.

Directions Ask: Which source would be best to find out how to get a library card? Have children circle the best source and then tell why.

 School + Home

Home Activity Discuss with your child ways that the computer can be a good source for information .

Name _____

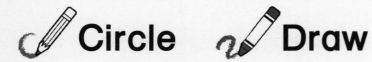 Circle Draw

☆ DAILY STAR ☆
Tallahassee and Ft. Worth
win recycling awards.

Directions Ask: Which source or sources would you use to find the hours the library is open? Have children circle the best source(s). In the empty space, have them draw another source they could use to answer the question. Discuss their choices.

Home Activity Suggest various types of information and have your child tell where to look for the information.

Name _____

 Write  Color

__ilt__

__ak__

Yy
Qq

__arn__

__ick__

__ack__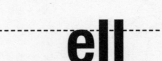

__ell__

© Pearson Education, Inc., K

 Directions: Name each picture. Write *y* if the word begins with /y/. Write *qu* if the word begins with /kw/. Color the /y/ pictures.

 Home Activity: Have your child draw pictures of things that begin with /y/ and /kw/.

Name _____

 Circle  Color

 Directions: Circle the picture that shows what you think the child would do next. Color the pictures.

 Home Activity: Have your child explain how he or she arrived at each conclusion.

392 **Comprehension** Draw Conclusions

© Pearson Education, Inc., K

Name _____

 Circle  Write

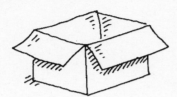

The box is big.

_____
- - - - - - - - - - - - - -
_____

The bus will go fast.

_____
- - - - - - - - - - - - - -
_____

That is a big bed.

_____
- - - - - - - - - - - - - -
_____

 Directions Say the picture name. Read the sentence.
Circle the noun. Then write the noun on the lines.

 Home Activity Point to and read sentences in a book.
Have your child identify the nouns.

Conventions Nouns in Sentences **393**

© Pearson Education, Inc., K

Name _____

✏️ Write   🖍 Draw

1. _____

_____

2. _____

_____

3. _____

_____

 Directions Have children write, dictate, or copy their draft or key words from the how-to report. Have them draw pictures to go with the list.

 Home Activity Ask your child to tell you what he or she learned about the topic of the class how-to report.

394 Writing Process Drafting

Name _____

 Circle  **Color**

pets

animals

plants

animals

 Directions: Circle the word that tells what the
pictures in the row are all about. Color the pictures.

 Home Activity: Have your child tell what each set of
pictures is all about.

Comprehension Main Idea   **395**

Name _____

 Circle  **Write**

sat

bat

_____

- - - - - - - - - - - - - - - -

The man _____ here.

mop

hop

_____

- - - - - - - - - - - - - - - -

Jan can _____ .

jump

dump

_____

- - - - - - - - - - - - - - - -

Pat can _____ .

looks

hooks

_____

- - - - - - - - - - - - - - - -

Nan _____ at it.

fan

ran

_____

- - - - - - - - - - - - - - - -

The man _____ fast.

likes

bikes

_____

- - - - - - - - - - - - - - - -

Tom _____ the bird.

 Directions: Look at the picture. Circle the verb that completes the sentence. Then write the word and read the sentence.

 Home Activity: Have your child use the verb that is not circled in each box in a sentence.

Name _____

✏️ Write 🖍️ Draw

I will add this to my draft.

_____

- -

_____

- -

_____

Directions Have children draw pictures of and write or dictate additional details and sentences that could be included in the how-to report.

 Home Activity Have your child tell you how the class revised the how-to report to make it better.

Writing Process Revising **397**

Name _____

 Write 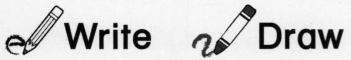 Draw

_____

- -

_____

_____

- -

_____

_____

- -

_____

 Directions Have children draw, write, or dictate the entire how-to report.

 Home Activity Discuss with your child another topic he or she would like to write about. Try drafting a how-to report on this topic.

Name _____

 Circle    Write

I. how doyou do it

_____

- - - - - - - - - - - - - - - - - - - -

_____

2. first, sign   up for a card

_____

- - - - - - - - - - - - - - - - - - - -

_____

3. Last, show   your newcard

_____

- - - - - - - - - - - - - - - - - - - -

_____

 Directions Have children circle the mistakes and rewrite the words or sentences correctly on the lines.

 Home Activity Have your child point out and explain his or her edits.

Name _____

 Circle  Write

_____

- -

I shared my selection with _____.

Here's what he/she learned.

_____

- -

_____

_____

 Directions Have children circle the picture that shows with whom they shared their how-to report. Then have children ask the peer or adult reviewer to fill in the blanks and to discuss the how-to report with him or her.

 School + Home **Home Activity** Ask your child to read or tell the how-to report to you.

Name _____

✏️ Write

A

a

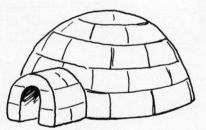

I

i

_____
- - - - - - - - - - - - - - - - - - - -
_____

_____
- - - - - - - - - - - - - - - - - - - -
_____

_____
- - - - - - - - - - - - - - - - - - - -
_____

_____
- - - - - - - - - - - - - - - - - - - -
_____

cat _____
- - - - - - - - - - -
_____

pig _____
- - - - - - - - - - - - - - - - -
_____

🍎 **Directions** Have children write a row of each letter and then write the words.

School + Home **Home Activity** Ask your child to write each letter and tell you how to make the letter.

Handwriting Letters *A,a* and *I,i*: Words with *a* and *i*   **401**

Name _____

 Write  Color

_____   _____

m   t      **p   n**

_____   _____

c   b      **k   t**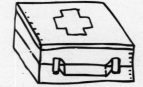

Aa
Ii

_____   _____

p   g      **j   m**

 Directions: Name each picture. Write *a* or *i* to finish each word. Color the /a/ pictures.

School + Home **Home Activity:** Have your child write *tin* and *tan* and draw a picture for each word.

402   Phonics Review /a/, /i/

Vin will zip the bag.

He and the bag will go on a trip.

4

Vin and the Bag

Vin had a bag.

The bag is a big bag.

1

He got one big can.

He got one little net.

He got one little kit.

He got one big rag.

Name _____

 Write  Color

what   with   do   little

_____

- -
_____ you like to jump?

_____

- -
I will go _____ you.

_____

- -
My dog is _____ .

_____

- -
_____ can I do to help?

© Pearson Education, Inc., K

 **Directions:** Write the missing word to finish each sentence. Color the pictures.

School + Home **Home Activity:** Have your child use the high-frequency words in other sentences.

High-Frequency Words 405

Name _____

 **Read It!**

I have a pet.

The pet is for me.

Say It!

Tell about something you have using the words **I** and **me**.

 **Write It!**

_____

_____ have a ball. (I)

_____

The ball is for _____ . (me)

 Directions Have children track the print and read the sentences about the pet. Ask them to say sentences for things they have using *I* and *me*. Then have children write the pronouns *I* and *me* to complete the sentences.

406 Conventions Pronouns *I* and *Me*

 Home Activity Have your child read the sentences and find the pronouns *I* and *me*. Then have him or her create other sentences with the pronouns *I* and *me*.

© Pearson Education, Inc., K

Name _____

 Write  Color

_____

- - - - - - - - - - - - - - - - - - -

_____

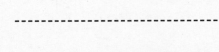

_____

- - - - - - - - - - - - - - - - - - -

_____

Directions: Say the word that names the picture. Spell the picture name. Write the word on the lines. Color the /i/ pictures.

 Home Activity: Have your child draw a picture of something with /i/. Then help him or her spell and write the picture name.

Name _____

 Color

Directions: Color the picture that is different in each row.

School + Home

Home Activity: Have your child tell how the pictures are alike and how they are different.

© Pearson Education, Inc., K

408 Comprehension Compare and Contrast

Name _____

 Circle  Write

Rob zips the bag up.

_____
- -
_____

Jill ran with the net.

_____
- -
_____

Tim pats the little pet.

_____
- -
_____

 Directions Read the sentence about the picture.
Circle the verb. Then write the verb on the lines.
Then say a sentence using the verb.

 Home Activity Point to and read sentences in a book.
Have your child identify the verb in each sentence.

Name _____

✏️ # Write

🍎 **Directions** Write or dictate a list of things from *Building with Dad* that you want to learn more about.

🏫 School + Home **Home Activity** Help your child write a list of toys he or she knows how to use.

Name _____

 Circle  Color

 Directions: Circle the picture in the third box to tell what Carl eats. Color the pictures. Circle the picture in the third box to tell how Rosa gets to Australia. Color the pictures.

 Home Activity: Have your child tell why he or she drew each conclusion.

Comprehension Draw Conclusions **411**

Name _____

 # Read It!

I have a book.

The book is for me.

Say It!

Tell about something you have using the words **I** and **me**.

 # Write It!

_____

_____ have a hat. (I)

_____

The hat is for _____ . (me)

 Directions Have children read the sentences about the book. Ask them to say sentences for things they have using *I* and *me*. Then have children write the pronouns *I* and *me* to complete the sentences.

 Home Activity Have your child create sentences with the pronouns *I* and *me*.

© Pearson Education, Inc., K

Name _____

✏️ **Write**

_____
- -
_____

_____
- -
_____

top ------------------------------
_____

fox ------------------------------
_____

🍎 **Directions:** Have children write a row of each letter and then write the words.

🏫 School + Home **Home Activity:** Ask your child to show you how to write each letter.

Name _____

 Write    Color

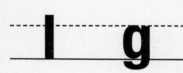 l g

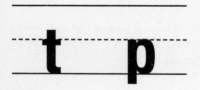 t p    Aa

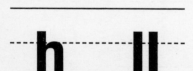 h ll    Ii Oo

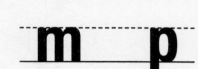 m p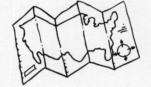

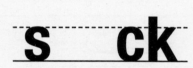 s ck

 p t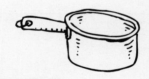

 Directions: Write *a*, *i*, or *o* to finish each word. Color the /o/ pictures.

School + Home   **Home Activity:** Have your child write *lock* and *rock* and draw a picture for each word.

Dad will spin the top.

Dad can spin it.

Dad can get the top
to spin.

4

Spin the Top

Bob got a top.

Bob will spin the top.

1

The top will not spin.

The top will not go.

Help! Help!

Help me spin the top.

It will not spin.

Help! Help!

Name _____

 Write  Color

| where | go | that | come |

_____

- - - - - - - - - - - - - - - - - -

I will _____ with you.

_____

- - - - - - - - - - - - - - - - - -

I can _____ with you.

_____

- - - - - - - - - - - - - - - - - -

Did you see _____ ?

_____

- - - - - - - - - - - - - - - - - -

_____ do you live?

🍎 **Directions:** Read each sentence. Write the missing word to finish the sentence. Color the picture.

School + Home **Home Activity:** Have your child use *where, go, that,* and *come* in other sentences.

Name _____

 **Read It!**

The cat is on the box.

Say It!

Say a sentence about a dog using the phrase **in the box.**

 **Write It!**

_____

The dog sat _____ (by the book).

 Directions Have children track the print and read the sentence with you. Ask them to say a sentence with the phrase *in the box.* Have children write the prepositional phrase to complete the sentence.

 Home Activity Have your child create sentences using the prepositional phrases *on the table, in the sink,* or *on the bed.*

418 **Conventions** Prepositional Phrases

Name _____

 Write  Color

_____

- - - - - - - - - - - - - - - - - -

_____

_____

- - - - - - - - - - - - - - - - - -

_____

_____

- - - - - - - - - - - - - - - - - -

_____

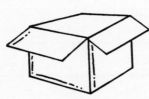

_____

- - - - - - - - - - - - - - - - - -

_____

_____

- - - - - - - - - - - - - - - - - -

_____

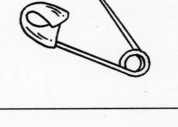

_____

- - - - - - - - - - - - - - - - - -

_____

 Directions: Say the word that names the picture. Spell the picture name. Write the word on the lines. Color the /o/ pictures.

 Home Activity: Have your child draw a picture of something with /o/. Then help him or her spell and write the picture name.

Name _____

 Draw 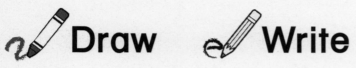 Write

 Directions: Draw your favorite character from *Old MacDonald had a Woodshop*, and then write or dictate words describing it.

 Home Activity: Talk about the favorite character your child drew and have your child describe it.

420 **Comprehension** Character

Name _____

Read It!

I got a top.

The top is for me.

Say It!

Tell about something you have using the words **I** and **me**.

Write It!

_____

- -

_____ have a toy car. (I)

_____

- - - - - - - - - - - - - - - - - - - -

The toy car is for _____. (me)

Directions Have children track the print and read the sentences with you. Ask them to say sentences for things they have using *I* and *me*. Then have children write the pronouns *I* and *me* to complete the sentences.

Home Activity Have your child read the sentences and find the pronouns *I* and *me*. Then have him or her create other sentences with the pronouns *I* and *me*.

Name _____

 Write Draw

Old MacDonald had a farm, E-I-E-I-O.

_____

And on his farm he had a _____

 Directions Have children complete the song about Old MacDonald by writing or dictating a kind of animal. Then have each child draw a picture of the animal he or she chose.

 Home Activity Help your child create another verse for the "Old MacDonald Had a Farm" song.

Name _____

 **Draw**

 Directions: Draw a picture to show what would happen next in each story.

 School + Home **Home Activity:** With your child, retell a familiar story. You begin the story and ask your child to tell what happens next.

Name _____

 **Read It!**

The bug is in the tub.

Say It!

Say a sentence using the phrase **on the window.**

 Write It!

_____

- -

The bug ran _____ (on the rug).

Directions Have children track the print and read the sentence with you. Ask them to use the phrase *on the window* in a sentence. Then have children write the prepositional phrase *on the rug* to complete the sentence.

School + Home

Home Activity Have your child create sentences using the prepositional phrases *on the chair, in the book,* or *under the couch.*

424 **Conventions** Prepositional Phrases

Name _____

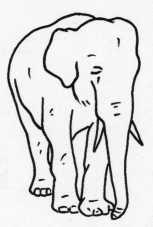

✏️ Write

_____

- -

_____

- -

_____

Ed - - - - - - - - - - - - - - -
_____

pet - - - - - - - - - - - - - - -
_____

🍎 **Directions:** Have children write a row of each letter and then write the words.

 School + Home **Home Activity:** Ask your child to show you how to write each letter.

Handwriting Letters *E, e: Words with e* **425**

Name _____

 Write    Color

_____
w   **b**

h   **t**

Aa
Ee
Ii

_____
l   **g**

m   **n**

_____
p   **n**

j   **t**

 Directions: Write *a*, *i*, or *e* for each word. Color the /e/ pictures.

School + Home **Home Activity:** Have your child write *hen* and *pen* and draw a picture for each word.

The hen had little ones.

Jim and Kim have lots of little hens.

4

Decodable Story *Jim and Kim*
Target Skill Review

Jim and Kim

Jim and Kim had a pet.

They had a pet hen.

The hen was in a pen.

1

Jim had fun with the pet hen.

Jim fed the hen.

Kim had fun with the pet hen.

Kim got a nest for the hen.

Name _____

 Write  Color

| was | like | the | from |

_____

This is _____ big pet.

_____

I _____ to run fast.

_____

The box is _____ him.

_____

I _____ the best one for the job.

© Pearson Education, Inc., K

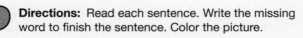 **Directions:** Read each sentence. Write the missing word to finish the sentence. Color the picture.

 Home Activity: Have your child use *was, like, the* and *from* in other sentences.

Name _____

 **Write**  **Color**

is   big   flag   the

_____

- - - - - - - - - - - - - - - - - -

_____

a   has   pet   he

_____

- - - - - - - - - - - - - - - - - -

_____

on   sits   she   a   box

_____

- - - - - - - - - - - - - - - - - -

_____

run   fast   can   I

_____

- - - - - - - - - - - - - - - - - -

_____

 Directions: Use the words in each box to write a sentence about the picture. Remember to use an uppercase letter and a period. Color the pictures.

 Home Activity: Have your child read each sentence.

Name _____

 Write  Color

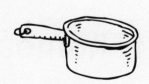

_____
- - - - - - - - - - -
_____

_____
- - - - - - - - - - -
_____

_____
- - - - - - - - - - -
_____

_____
- - - - - - - - - - -
_____

_____
- - - - - - - - - - -
_____

_____
- - - - - - - - - - -
_____

Directions: Say the word that names the picture. Spell the picture name. Write the word on the lines. Color the /e/ pictures.

 School + Home

Home Activity: Have your child draw a picture of something with /e/. Then help him or her spell and write the picture name.

Phonics Review /a/, /e/, /o/ **431**

Name _____

 **Circle**

pets

tools

homes

 Directions: Have children give information about each picture. Then ask them to circle that word that tells main idea or topic shown in the pictures.

 Home Activity: Have your child tell about each picture.

432 **Comprehension** Main Idea

Name _____

 Read It!

The hen is in the pen.

Say It!

Say a sentence about an animal using the phrase **under the tree.**

 **Write It!**

_____

- -

The duck is _____ (on the leaf).

 Directions Have children track the print and read the sentence with you. Ask them to say a sentence with the phrase *under the tree.* Then have children write the prepositional phrase to complete the sentence.

 Home Activity Have your child create sentences using the prepositional phrases *on the table* and *in the sink.*

Conventions Prepositional Phrases   **433**

Name _____

✏️ Write   🖍️ Draw

_____
- -
_____
- -
_____

 Directions Have children copy the rhyme they created about the beavers. Then have them draw a picture of the beaver.

 Home Activity Help your child make a rhyme about an animal and draw the animal's picture.

Name _____

 Draw  Color

 Directions: Draw a line from what happened to why it happened. Color each picture.

 Home Activity: Have your child tell you what happened in each picture in the first row and why it happened.

Comprehension Cause and Effect **435**

Name _____

 **Write**  **Color**

is   bug   the   big

_____

- - - - - - - - - - - - - - - - -

got   she   a   pet

_____

- - - - - - - - - - - - - - - - -

here   hen   a   sat

_____

- - - - - - - - - - - - - - - - -

fast   dog   the   ran

_____

- - - - - - - - - - - - - - - - -

 Directions Use the words to write a sentence about the picture. Remember to use an uppercase letter and a period. Color the pictures.

 Home Activity Have your child read each sentence.

436 **Conventions** Telling Sentences

Name _____

 Write

sun _____

cup _____

Directions: Have children write a row of each letter and then write the words.

 School + Home **Home Activity:** Ask your child to show you how to write each letter.

Name _____

 Write    Color

_____
s _____ **n**

_____
c _____ **p**

_____
b _____ **s**

Aa
Oo
Uu

_____
b _____ **t**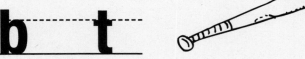

_____
p _____ **p**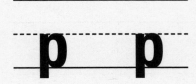

_____
c _____ **t**

 Directions: Write *a*, *o*, or *u* to finish each word. Color the /u/ pictures.

School + Home **Home Activity:** Have your child write *hut* and *nut* and draw a picture for each word.

Gus grabs the bug.

Gus lets the bug go.

4

Gus and the Bug

Gus will hug his mom.

Gus gets on the bus.

1

Gus sat with his pal Wes.

The sun was hot.

A bug got on the bus.

It sat with Gus and Wes.

Name _____

 **Write**    **Color**

of   my   yellow   we

_____

This is _____ big pet.

_____
The sun is _____.

_____

_____ like to jump.

_____

Here are two _____ my hats.

Directions: Write the missing word to finish each sentence. Color the pictures.

School + Home   **Home Activity:** Have your child use the high-frequency words in other sentences.

Name _____

 **Draw**

Where is the cat?

Do you see the dog?

What did the bug do?

Can you see me?

The bug ran to see me.

I can not see you.

The cat is here.

I can see the dog.

 Directions: Read each question and the answer choices aloud. Then draw a line from each question to its answer.

 Home Activity: Ask your child the questions and have him or her create an answer using a complete sentence.

442 **Conventions** Questions

Name _____

 Write  Color

_____

- - - - - - - - - - - - - - -

_____

_____

- - - - - - - - - - - - - - -

_____

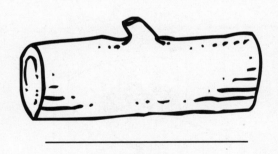

_____

- - - - - - - - - - - - - - -

_____

_____

- - - - - - - - - - - - - - -

_____

_____

- - - - - - - - - - - - - - -

_____

 Directions: Say the word that names the picture. Spell the picture name. Write the word on the lines. Color the /u/ pictures.

 Home Activity: Have your child draw a picture of something with /u/. Then help him or her spell and write the picture name.

Phonics Review /a/, /e/, /o/, /u/ **443**

Name _____

 Color

 Directions: Color the picture that shows what would happen next in each story.

 Home Activity: Have your child tell you the story of *Alistair and Kip's Great Adventure*.

444 Comprehension Plot

Name _____

 **Write**   **Color**

wet   pup   the   got

_____

- - - - - - - - - - - - - - - - - - - -

boy   the   sad   is

_____

- - - - - - - - - - - - - - - - - - - -

girl   fast   the   went

_____

- - - - - - - - - - - - - - - - - - - -

is   the   nut   big

_____

- - - - - - - - - - - - - - - - - - - -

© Pearson Education, Inc., K

 Directions Use the words in each box to write a sentence about the picture. Remember to use an uppercase letter and a period. Color the pictures.

School + Home **Home Activity** Have your child read each sentence.

Conventions Telling Sentences   **445**

Name _____

✎ Write   🖍 Draw

_____
- -
_____
- -
_____

 Directions Have children say the rhyme they created about Alistair and Kip's boat trip. Then have them write the rhyme and draw a picture of the trip.

 Home Activity Help your child make a rhyme about a trip and draw a picture to tell more about the trip.

446 **Writing** Rhyme

Name _____

Circle ✏ Color 🖍

PETS

Directions: Circle the picture in the top right box to tell how Ann gets to school. Color the pictures. Circle the picture in the bottom right box to tell which kitten Joe gets. Color the pictures.

School + Home

Home Activity: Have your child tell why he or she drew each conclusion.

Comprehension Draw Conclusions **447**

Name _____

 **Draw**

Where is the pup?

I can see the bus.

Can you see the bus?

The hen is not little.

What can the cat do?

The pup is here.

Is the hen little?

The cat can run.

 Directions Read each question and the answer choices aloud. Then draw a line from each question to its answer.

 School + Home **Home Activity** Use these question frames and add a household item: *Is the ___ big? Where is the ___?* Ask your child to repeat the question and give an answer. Then have your child create questions for you to answer.

448 **Conventions** Questions

Name _____

 Write

 pen _____

 cat _____

 bus _____

 pin _____

 dog _____

 pan _____

 Directions Have children write each word. Then have them read the words together.

 Home Activity Ask your child to show you how to write each word.

Handwriting Words **449**

© Pearson Education, Inc., K

Name _____

 Circle  Color

 leg log	 pen pan	 pep pup
 bag beg	 led lid	 tub tab

 Directions: Circle the word that names the picture.
Color the pictures.

School + Home **Home Activity:** Have your child use the words in
sentences.

What Pets Do

Peg is a dog.

She will tug.

She will dig.

Sam is a cat.

Sam will sit in a lap.

He will nap.

4

1

Hal is a pet pig.

He will run in his pen.

He will go in the mud.

2

Tad is a pet frog.

He will hop.

He will swim.

3

Name _____

 Write  Color

| blue | they | have | four |

_____

Do I still look _____?

_____

The bed is _____.

_____

We can _____ fun.

_____

_____ play with a ball.

 Directions: Read each sentence. Write the missing
word to finish the sentence. Color the picture.

 Home Activity: Have your child use the
high-frequency words in other sentences.

High-Frequency Words 453

Name _____

 Circle  **Write**

Can I swim _____

Yes, I can -

_____

I am glad _____

Is the pig big -

_____

Is he sad _____

Help me -

_____

 Directions Circle the sentence that is an exclamation. Write the sentence. Use an exclamation mark.

School + Home **Home Activity** Have your child read each exclamation and point to the exclamation mark.

Name _____

 Write  Color

- - - - - - - - - - - - - - - - - - -

- - - - - - - - - - - - - - - - - - -

- - - - - - - - - - - - - - - - - - -

- - - - - - - - - - - - - - - - - - -

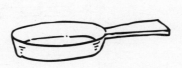

- - - - - - - - - - - - - - - - - - -

- - - - - - - - - - - - - - - - - - -

© Pearson Education, Inc., K

Directions: Name each picture and spell the picture name. Write the word on the lines. Then color the pictures that rhyme.

 School + Home

Home Activity: Have your child use the picture names in sentences.

Phonics Review /a/, /e/   **455**

Name _____

 Color

MOVING
VAN

Directions: Color the picture that shows the setting
of the story *The House That Tony Lives In*.

 Home Activity: Have your child tell you when and
where the story takes place.

Name _____

 **Draw**

What did they do?   She did the plans.

What did she do?   They built things.

What did he do?   They talked to us.

What did they do?   He planted things.

 Directions Read each question and the answer choices aloud. Then draw a line from each question to its answer.

 School + Home

Directions Have your child read each question to you. Then help him or her write a new question.

Name _____

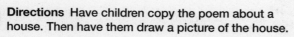 Write    Draw

_____

- -

_____

- -

_____

 Directions Have children copy the poem about a house. Then have them draw a picture of the house.

School + Home **Home Activity** Help your child make a poem with rhyming words such as *rug, bug, tug, dug, hug, jug,* and *mug*.

458 **Writing** Poem

Name _____

 Circle  Color

Directions: Circle the make-believe pictures. Color
the real pictures.

 Home Activity: With your child, look at a book about
how real animals live.

Name _____

 Circle   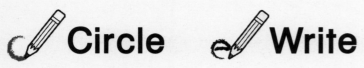 Write

Can you run fast   _____

I ran fast   -
_____

I like it   _____

Will I get a pet   -
_____

So you like my pet   _____

That was fun   -
_____

 Directions Circle the sentence that is an exclamation.
Write the sentence. Use an exclamation mark.

School + Home **Home Activity** Have your child read each exclamation
and point to the exclamation mark.

460 Conventions Exclamations

Name _____

 Write

 cap _____

 log _____

 net _____

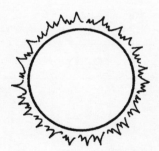 sun _____

 pig _____

 web _____

 Directions Have children write each word. Then have them read the words together.

 Home Activity Ask your child to show you how to write each word.

Name _____

 **Draw**

pin 　　cub 　　hut

pen 　　cab 　　hat

pan 　　cob 　　hit

 Directions: Draw lines to match the words with the pictures.

 Home Activity: Have your child draw pictures for these words: *cat, cot, cut.*

Name _____

What Can You Do?

Here is Ned.

Ned can run fast.

Ned can run and run.

1

I am Jen.

I can hang from my legs.

What can you do?

4

Decodable Story *What Can You Do?*
Target Skill Review

Look at Ken.

He fed the big dog.

He fed the little dogs.

2

See Kim jump.

She can go from me to you.

She can jump from here to here.

3

Name _____

 **Draw**

 Directions Have children draw pictures of animals as report topic ideas.

 Home Activity Ask your child to tell you about his or her pictures of topic ideas.

Name _____

 Draw   Write

_____

- -

_____

- -

_____

Directions Have children illustrate or write the class research topic question and dictate or write another question about the topic.

 Home Activity Ask your child to tell you about the report the class is planning to write.

Name _____

 Write  Color

| three | said | look | you |

_____

- - - - - - - - - - - - - - - - - - -

_____ at that bug.

_____

- - - - - - - - - - - - - - - - - - - -

Do _____ like hot dogs?

_____

- - - - - - - - - - - - - - - - - - -

I _____ I will run fast.

_____

- - - - - - - - - - - - - - - - - - - -

I have _____ cats.

Directions: Read each sentence. Write the missing word to finish the sentence. Color the picture.

 Home Activity: Have your child use the high-frequency words in other sentences.

Name _____

 **Draw**

The big dog

One doll

The man

A little pig

was on the bed.

had a little pup.

sat in the mud.

sat in the den.

 Directions: Draw lines to make complete sentences. Say each sentence.

School + Home **Home Activity:** Ask your child to make new sentences using the sentence parts on the page.

Name _____

 Circle

Newspaper

Computer

Librarian

Television

Directions Ask: Which sources would you use to find out about animal homes? Have children circle the best source(s) for that information and then tell why.

 School + Home **Home Activity** Discuss with your child ways that a newspaper can be a good source of information.

Name _____

 Circle  Draw

Computer

Book

Radio

Directions Ask: Which sources would you use to find out what rabbits eat? Have children circle the best source(s) for that information. In the empty space, have them draw another source they could use to answer the question. Discuss their choices.

 Home Activity Suggest various types of information and have your child tell where to look for the information.

© Pearson Education, Inc., K

Name _____

 Write

_____

- - - - - - - - - - - - - - -

_____

_____

- - - - - - - - - - - - - - -

_____

_____

- - - - - - - - - - - - - - -

_____

_____

- - - - - - - - - - - - - - -

_____

_____

- - - - - - - - - - - - - - -

_____

_____

- - - - - - - - - - - - - - -

_____

_____

- - - - - - - - - - - - - - -

_____

 Directions: Name each picture and spell the picture name. Write the word on the lines.

School + Home **Home Activity:** Have your child write *mop* and *map* and draw a picture for each word.

Phonics Review /a/, /e/, /i/, /o/, /u/   **471**

Name _____

✏️ Circle

 Directions: Look at the animal home. Which animal would live in this home? Circle the animal.

 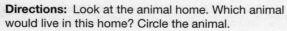 **Home Activity:** Have your child explain how he or she arrived at each conclusion.

Name _____

 **Write**

what a big bug

we went fast

we win

 Directions Read the words. Write the words to make an exclamation. Remember to use an exclamation mark at the end of the sentence.

 School + Home

Home Activity Help your child write other exclamations.

© Pearson Education, Inc., K

Name _____

Write   Draw

_____

1. _____

_____

2. _____

_____

3. _____

 Directions Have children write, dictate, or copy their draft or key words from the class report. Draw pictures for the words in your list.

 Home Activity Ask your child to tell you what he or she learned about the topic of the class report.

© Pearson Education, Inc., K

Name _____

 Color

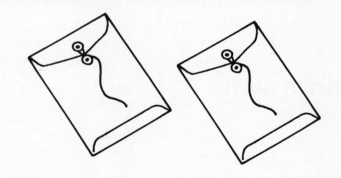

Directions: Color pairs of pictures that are alike.

School + Home **Home Activity:** Have your child tell how the pairs of pictures are alike or different.

Comprehension Compare and Contrast **475**

Name _____

Draw

I see the bus

We can see

The ants walk

The big hen is

the nest.

at the bus stop.

on the bed.

on the leaves.

 Directions Read the sentence parts. Draw lines to make complete sentences and read them.

 Home Activity Begin a sentence and have your child complete the sentence. Then take turns completing each other's sentences.

476 **Conventions** Complete Sentences

Name _____

 Draw 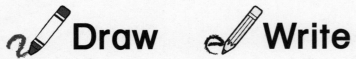 Write

I will add this to my draft.

_____

_____

_____

_____

 Directions Have children draw pictures of and write or dictate additional information that could be included in the class report.

 Home Activity Have your child tell you how the class revised the report to make it better.

Name _____

✎ Draw   ✏ Write

_____

- -

_____

_____

- -

_____

_____

- -

_____

Directions Have children draw, write, or dictate the entire class report.

Home Activity Discuss with your child another topic he or she would like to write about. Try drafting a report on this topic.

Name _____

 Circle  **Write**

1. a bird isin the nest.

_____

- -

_____

2. birds   usegrass

_____

- -

_____

3. we learnedabout   birds

_____

- -

_____

© Pearson Education, Inc., K

 Directions Have children circle the mistakes and rewrite the words or sentences correctly on the lines.

 School + Home **Home Activity** Have your child point out and explain his or her edits.

Name _____

 Circle  Write

_____

- -

I shared my selection with _____.

Here's what he / she learned.

_____

- -

_____

_____

- -

_____

 Directions Have children circle the picture that shows with whom they shared their report. Then have children ask the peer or adult reviewer to fill in the blanks and to discuss the report with him or her.

 Home Activity Ask your child to read or tell the class report to you.